Worksheets!

for Teaching Social Thinking and Related Skills

Breaking down concepts for teaching students with Social Cognitive Deficits.

*Includes: High Functioning Autism, Asperger Syndrome,
Nonverbal Learning Disability,
Attention Deficit Hyperactivity Disorder,
and whatever else fits!*

Michelle Garcia Winner, SLP

Published by Michelle Garcia Winner, SLP
Speech Language Pathologist, MA, CCC
3031 Tisch Way, Suite 800
San Jose, CA 95128
Telephone (408) 557-8595
Fax (408) 557-8594

1st Edition July 2005 • 3rd Printing March 2007
Copyright©2005 Michelle Garcia Winner, SLP
ISBN-13: 978-0-9701320-3-1
ISBN-10: 0-9701320-3-4

To order copies of this book or to learn about the workshops that Michelle presents, visit
www.socialthinking.com

Psychologists and Educators...

speak out about Michelle's new book:

"Michelle Winner's approach to addressing the needs of these students is the most innovative, practical, and exciting work I have learned in my 25 years as a Speech-Language Pathologist and Autism Specialist. This book, Worksheets, will allow you to spend less time planning and more time focusing on your students! This book is indispensable!"

Patty O'Meara, M.S., C.C.C.
Speech-Language Pathologist and Autism Specialist
Portland, Oregon

"This book contains very functional, practical, creative and fun strategies for the highly complex challenge of improving social relationships and enhancing life-long skills for many of our children, students and/or clients. Michelle makes it REALIZABLE, while teaching us new ways of looking at how we provide support to persons with 'Social Cognitive Deficits.' She not only has taught us to 'think with our eyes,' but to broaden our perspectives on how and what we teach. She is one of our favorite presenters, receiving OUTSTANDING evaluations from staff and parents alike!"

Andrea Walker, MA, Speech Pathologist
Coordinator, S.U.C.S.E.S.S. Project of Orange County, California
Orange County Department of Education

"A great collection of worksheets to help our students deepen their understanding of a variety of crucial social thinking concepts."

Lauren Franke Psy.D., CCC/SLP, Psychologist
Seal Beach, California

"Michelle again shares her passion...thinking about others...with awesome, thought provoking, hands on materials. My Navigating Social Dynamics groups are ready for more 'A-HA' moments with the help of her learning guides!"

Diane Taylor MS/CCC/SLP
Green Bay, Wisconsin

Introduction

The challenge in educating students with social thinking learning disabilities is that we need to teach them explicitly what most of us do intuitively. I have learned that in order to move our student's social knowledge and social skills forward, we need to break down abstract social concepts (such as talking on the telephone, making friends, planning a party, monitoring one's own social behavior, etc.) into small, concrete steps which help our students understand not only what skills to use but also why the skills should be used. In order to accomplish this goal, I often create worksheets to guide how I am going to introduce and work through specific lessons. While many of the worksheets appear to provide very basic concepts, it is important to understand how many of our seemingly intelligent students need information broken down far more than we may have first realized. I have amassed hundreds of these worksheets over the years; to save others from having to "reinvent the wheel," I have compiled many of them into this manual.

These worksheets complement many of the ideas discussed in my books, "Inside Out: What Makes A Person With Social Cognitive Deficits Tick?" and "Thinking About You Thinking About Me." They will also function as a useful companion to my "Social Thinking Curriculum" which is scheduled to be published during the 2005-2006 school year. In order to make the best use of the worksheets, users should first familiarize themselves with my philosophy and approach to addressing social-cognitive deficits by reading my books, attending my workshops, watching my DVD, and/or exploring the content posted on my website, www.socialthinking.com.

How the manual is organized

This manual is not intended to serve as a "curriculum" in and of itself. That is to say, the user should not start at page 1 and advance page by page through the manual with each student. Rather, therapists, educators and parents are encouraged to first generally familiarize themselves with the contents of this manual; then relevant worksheets can be chosen to facilitate the teaching of specific social thinking concepts and skills which have been identified as needed by the students they are working with. The worksheets are loosely organized into the following categories: "Learning About Our Own Behavior," "Self-Monitoring and Rating Sheets," "Friendships," "Being Part of a Group," "Exploring Language Concepts," "Developing Effective Communication," "Understanding and Interpreting Emotions," "Perspective Taking," "Making Plans to Be with Others," and "Problem Solving and Dealing with Responsibilities."

How to interpret the coding systems

The worksheets were developed for use with students from approximately the age of 6 through adulthood. The majority of worksheets are appropriate for students in mid-elementary school through high school. To help you identify age-appropriate worksheets for your students, a code appears in the top right hand corner of each worksheet which indicates the age group for which it is relevant. The codes are as follows:

- "A" indicates the worksheet is appropriate for children under 8 years of age.

- "B" indicates that the worksheet is appropriate for almost any age student, but it is particularly relevant for upper elementary school and middle school students.

- "C" indicates appropriateness for students of high school age through adulthood.

- "D" indicates that the worksheet was designed for the educator.

How to use the worksheets as part of a therapeutic lesson

I have attempted to make the worksheets self-explanatory in terms of how the lessons are intended to unfold. At our clinic we generally work through the lesson presented in a worksheet, and then facilitate play activities or discussions designed to further explore the concepts being taught. Typically at the end of our sessions, we invite parents in for a re-cap of what was taught that day. At that time we give parents copies of the worksheets to help them promote their children's generalization of the concepts at home and in the community. We always encourage parents to share the worksheets with the teachers and other professionals involved with their children and enlist their support, when possible, to further reinforce the concepts. I would encourage you to use and share these worksheets in a similar manner.

These worksheets would be an excellent addition to a "ME Binder" (discussed in the book, "Thinking About You Thinking About Me"). The "ME Binder" is a tool used to help students learn about their own specialized educational programs.

I believe these worksheets will help you learn how to make abstract social concepts accessible to your students by breaking them down into concrete, detailed lessons. I hope you enjoy using them and hope they will serve as a model for you to go on to generate other educational ideas and create more useful worksheets!

Acknowledgements

I have a tremendous group of clinicians who work with me at my clinic in San Jose, California, Michelle G. Winner's Center for Social Thinking. They have embraced these concepts, questioned them, and added to them with their own energy and insight. Many thanks to these women: Stephanie Madrigal, Randi Dodge, Deborah Hoffman, Sue Day, Amy Miller, Jamie Rivetts, and Reesa Feldsher.

While these worksheets and concepts look unassuming, a lot of work was poured into them by my friend and superb clinician, Chris Durbin. She took my "chicken scratch" worksheets and revised them as needed so that others could more easily interpret my ideas. Thank Chris if you find these concepts fairly easy to interpret!

My daughters, Heidi and Robyn, and their friends helped shape many of these worksheets by allowing me to observe what the teenage social world is supposed to look like. "Typical" teen social behavior is complex and very different from our adult interpretation of it!

A number of people behind the scenes at my office help advance my work in more ways than I can say. Thank you to Wilson Winner, Marilyn Dion, Dawnyelle Gardner, Benjamin Mika, and Cathy Hart. Without these people I would be stuck in the mud.

Finally, thank you to all of my clients, their families, and conference participants who have encouraged me over the years to keep developing new ideas and related written materials. Your enthusiasm and questions continue to fuel my work.

Contents

Section 1

Learning About Our Own Behavior

1

Learning About Our Own Behavior

When you work hard at learning to change a behavior, people notice!

When people see you working hard it changes how they feel about you.

When people feel good about how hard you are trying, they often want to do nice things for you, like give you a smile or some praise.

Sometimes when people have nice thoughts about you,
they say nice things like:

Good Job!!

Super Duper!!

WOW! Terrific!!

Sometimes they even let you earn a special treat.

What are some special treats you would like to earn at school for working hard on the behavior you are learning to control?

1. _____

2. _____

3. _____

Learning About Our Own Behavior

Be a Detective!

Write down the "unexpected behaviors" that you are working hard to change into "expected behaviors."

1. _____

2. _____

3. _____

Write down who you think would notice.

1. _____

2. _____

3. _____

4. _____

Later…

Write down how those people reacted when you did a great job working hard at the behaviors on your list.

What did they say or do?

_____

How did you make them feel?

_____

How did you feel when they treated you nicely?

_____

Learning About Our Own Behavior

3 Steps to Behavior Change

Now it's time to keep track of how well you are doing.

Every time you do an expected behavior that you are trying to do more of, someone will keep track of it. You do not have to start by keeping track of it yourself. One of your teachers can be the "tracker" at first. But for you to really learn to do the behavior all by yourself, you will have to learn to be your own "tracker."

If you are on step one of changing a behavior, this is called SELF-AWARENESS. During this step your teacher is the "tracker" of your success. This means that you are just learning to take some extra time to think about the behavior that you are trying to change. This step is all about THINKING; if your teacher talks to you about the behavior and sees that you are THINKING about it, then she will let you know you are on the road to learning to do it right.

If you are on step two of changing a behavior, this is called SELF-MONITORING. Your teacher or you can be the "tracker" now. This step combines "Thinking" and "Doing." When you self-monitor, you watch yourself by thinking about the unexpected behavior you are doing. When you think about it clearly and understand that it interrupts you or other people, then you want to try to control it. Each time you make that behavior go away, even a little bit, then you are self-monitoring. When you are self-monitoring, the unexpected behavior creeps in, and then you make it STOP.

If you are on step three, the final step of doing an expected behavior more often, then you are learning SELF-CONTROL. On this step you have become a really good detective and you can be your own tracker of the expected behavior. When you are showing self-control you are still THINKING about the behavior and you are really working hard to DO something differently! When you control a behavior, you don't let the unexpected behavior creep in to begin with!

Learning About Our Own Behavior

Page 4 of 8

3 Steps to Behavior Change Worksheet

Steps to Behavior Change	*How much help do I need to do this?*	Put a check in the box below that shows what step you are on.
1. SELF-AWARENESS	*My teacher keeps track of the behavior and reminds me to think about it.*	
2. SELF-MONITORING	*My teacher HELPS ME to keep track of my behavior.*	
3. SELF-CONTROL	*I keep track of my own behavior and notice that I don't do the unexpected behavior very much anymore.*	

Learning About Our Own Behavior

Page 5 of 8

Setting a GOAL and Working Toward IT

The behavior that I am working on is:

_____

You are helping yourself get better at doing this very specific behavior. You know what you need to do. And now you are ready to actually keep track of the behavior yourself. As you keep track of the behavior, you start to monitor it more closely and this helps you to change it.

How many times do you think you can control the behavior for each block of time in your schedule? _____ The number that you write is the goal you want to accomplish.

Put an "X" in a box for each time you were able to show some control over the behavior on the "Tracking My Goal Sheet" below. For example, put an "X" in the "One time!" box under MORNING the first time you controlled the behavior in the morning, an "X" in the "Two times" box the second time, etc. If you do a good job, your goal sheet should fill up with Xs!

TRACKING MY GOAL SHEET

Name _____   Date _____

	MORNING	RECESS	AFTER RECESS	LUNCH	AFTERNOON
Ten times!!!!!					
Nine times!					
Eight times!					
Seven times!					
Six times!					
Five times!					
Four times!					
Three times!					
Two times!					
One time!					

You should be really, really proud of yourself for working at this, even if you have not yet met your goal!

© Michelle Garcia Winner 2005 • www.socialthinking.com

Learning About Our Own Behavior

"Tracking My Goals" Day after Day

I have been monitoring and tracking a specific behavior for one day. Now I want to try to see if I can do that day after day. The more I practice the behavior, the less I have to think about it. The more I do the behavior, the more it becomes part of me.

My teacher will give me the same "Tracking My Goal" sheet to use every day. Then each day I should think about the behavior I am changing, monitor it, and try to control it.

Goals require me to THINK about what I want to do. Then I have to PLAN for how to meet my goal. And then I have to CARRY OUT my plan. When I have done all of that, I will have MET MY GOAL!

When I meet my goal people definitely notice! If I do even better than my goal, people are really, really proud of me. Even better than that... I am really proud of myself!

Once I meet a goal, I start deciding how I can help myself to change another behavior. I know that even adults keep trying to change little things about how they behave.

For behaviors that are harder for me, I will set smaller goals so people will notice sooner just how hard I am working to do the behavior right.

As a behavior gets easier for me, then I will set bigger and bigger goals. When I can finally self-control my behavior, I get the biggest reward of all -- knowing that I can take care of myself!...one behavior at a time... day after day.

Learning About Our Own Behavior

Just when things are going right, I get all mixed up!

On some days it is easier to do what people expect,
and on other days it is harder.
That's OK!

The harder days are called "waking up on the wrong side of the bed."

Having one of these days every once in a while is OK.

But you have to work even harder on those days.

When the work gets too hard, it is OK to have a break and have a quiet moment to yourself. Sometimes you need a quiet moment to get yourself calm and able to focus on the behaviors for learning.

It is best to ask for a quiet moment BEFORE you get too stressed out.

Learning About Our Own Behavior

Page 8 of 8

Planning for a Bad Moment in the Day

When I start to feel stressed, my parents and teachers have agreed that I should do the following plan.

1. I need to tell people how I am feeling either by talking or by showing them a picture or word that explains it. The people I can talk to include:

   _____

   _____

2. I need to let them know that I need to change something that I am doing. Sometimes this means I need to go to a quieter place away from all the other people. I know that I still need an adult to be near me, but one adult is a lot better than a whole roomful of confusing people. A quiet place I can go to is:

   _____

3. When I am in the quieter place, I need to use some strategies to help me calm down. The strategies that help me the most are:

   a. _____

   b. _____

   c. _____

4. Once I am calm, I want to rejoin the group. When I rejoin the group I know there will be things I am expected to do that I may not want to do. But when I do those things, then I really am part of the group! Many other students in school also get bored or don't understand why they have to do an assignment. They do it anyway to help the group work. Groups only work well when the people in the group work together. When I am successfully part of a group, more people want to play with me and they help me to feel important.

Self–Monitor!

Identify an "unexpected behavior" that you do and consider how you can replace it with an "expected" behavior.

I need to increase my awareness of:
(Name the behavior.)

_____

I can monitor my behavior by thinking about it.
When I think about it, I can control it!

I WILL try to better CONTROL MY behavior by:
(describe a strategy to use)

_____

11

Self-Awareness, Self-Monitoring, and Self-Control

Refer to pages 4 and 5

Name_____   Date_____

I need to try to get better at *(name a behavior)* _____

_____

because_____

_____

_____

1. I am self-aware when I _____

_____

_____

2. I will self-monitor myself when _____

_____

_____

3. I can use self-control by _____

_____

_____

Reviewing How to Change a Single Behavior

Refer to pages 4 and 5

There are three steps you have to go through to change a single behavior:

1. Self- _____

Describe it.

_____

_____

2. Self-_____

Describe it.

_____

_____

3. Self-_____

Describe it.

_____

_____

There are so many behaviors each of us could work on, but it works better if we only try to change 2 or 3 at a time! Nobody's even close to perfect, ever!

List the behavior or behaviors you are trying to learn to control right now:

_____

_____

(Put a star next to the step you are working on.)

Modifying My Own Behaviors, One by One!

Moving mountains is hard; moving piles of dirt is much easier. But if you move enough piles of dirt, eventually the mountain moves too! The same thing happens with modifying our behaviors. If we can modify just one small behavior at a time, then after a while this can add up to "moving a mountain."

Today you will focus on ONE behavior you can do differently when you leave the therapy session and go home to your REAL life.

Thinking ALWAYS comes before doing.
What is one behavior you can think about in your brain that you would like to modify?

_____

Wanting to modify a behavior and actually doing it are two different things. What is ONE thing you will do differently with your body to change the behavior this week? *(Don't forget, we still don't expect you to do it right all the time!)*

_____

Now that you have agreed to investigate modifying this behavior, we expect a full report to the group about when it was easier and when it was harder to do the behavior change when you come to group next week. You can count on it!

Different Behaviors in Different Places

How are your behaviors expected to be different in different places?

Compare your behaviors at home and at school.

Home: _____

School: _____

Compare your behaviors at therapy to that in a doctor's waiting room.

Therapy Office: _____

Doctor's Waiting Room: _____

Why is your behavior expected to be different in different places?

_____

_____

_____

Discuss this with your group.

Different Behaviors Are Expected
at Different Times

Name_____ Date_____

Students can not be "good" by acting exactly the same way everywhere they go. Make some smart guesses about what different people expect of your behaviors in the following situations.

1. Your peers at school during break, lunch time, and relaxed times in class:
_____
_____

2. Your teachers during class time: _____
_____

3. Your parents at home: _____
_____

4. Your siblings at home: _____
_____

5. Your friends away from school: _____
_____

It is important to realize that the rules for our behaviors change in different places and at different times of the day. These rules are called the "hidden rules" because people don't talk much about them. We need to observe and figure out how the rules change in different places.

*Activity: Go to various places on the school campus and describe how the rules differ depending on the situation.

What Can You Do to Help Yourself?

List your strengths in dealing with new people or new situations.	List your weaknesses when dealing with new people or new situations.

What behavior(s) do you think would help you to be a more cooperative person in the following situations:

a. in the classroom? _____

b. During free-time at school? _____

c. When things change in your schedule? _____

d. When you are at home? _____

What do you think your parents are most concerned about:

a. When it comes to you and school? _____
_____

b. When it comes to you and home? _____
_____

What decisions are your parents making to try to help you? _____
_____
_____

Do you understand their decisions? Explain why or why not. _____
_____
_____

What Do People Expect?

People expect you to:

    1. Behave... What does that mean?

    2. Communicate... What does that mean?

But, how you are expected to behave and communicate is different in different places!
What do people expect from you:

    1. In the classroom?

    2. At recess?

    3. At the dinner table at home?

    4. At home when you are playing?

    5. At home when it is bedtime?

    6. When you are visiting someone's office?

How do people feel if you behave or talk in a way that people expect you to?

How do people feel if you behave or talk in a way that is surprising to them (unexpected)?

My Tools for Building a ME
That Works Well with YOU!

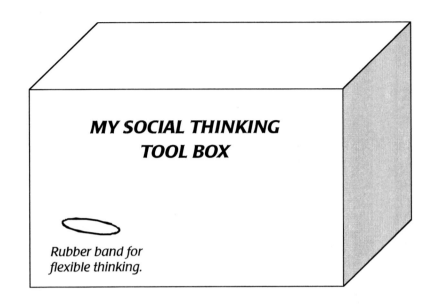

Write or draw tools in the box that you can use to help you be a better social thinker.

1. A rubber band to be a flexible thinker!

2. _____

3. _____

4. _____

5. _____

6. _____

Making a Behavior Plan for Yourself

Page 1 of 2

Name _____ Date _____

When you adjust a behavior you:
- Increase the time you think about the behavior.
- Increase opportunities to observe the behavior.
- Increase opportunities to use the behavior.
- Increase use of the behavior to make others feel good in your presence.

What are two small things you can ADJUST (which means "change") to help you work toward your plan?

Behavior Plan:

List the two behaviors you are trying to adjust:	Where do you plan to do this?	How many times per day do you plan to do it?
1._____ _____ _____ Describe why it is important to adjust this behavior. _____ _____		
2._____ _____ _____ Describe why it is important to adjust this behavior. _____ _____		

Making a Behavior Plan for Yourself: How Did You Do?

Page 2 of 2

Evaluation questions to ask yourself:

How many times per day were you able to do each behavior?

How did others feel when you did the behaviors?

When you do new behaviors that help you and others work together more positively, how do people treat you differently?

_____

_____

_____

_____

_____

Idea taken from: CEC Journal Volume 69 #4, Summer 2003 pages 431-447

21

Behaviors for Learning

Page 1 of 2

All things we do with our bodies, eyes, hands, feet, arms, and words are called "behaviors."

Certain behaviors actually help us learn from people and things (like books) that are around us everyday, both at school and at home.

I bet you know what some of these are. Let's see...

What should you do with your ears when the teacher is talking?

_____

What should you do with your eyes when the teacher is talking?

_____

What should you do with your feet when you are sitting and the teacher is talking?

_____

What should you do with your bottom when you are supposed to be sitting and listening?

_____

What should you do with your mouth and voice when other kids are listening to the teacher?

_____

What should your brain think about when the teacher is talking?

_____

What should you do when someone else is acting silly while the teacher is talking?

_____

What should you do when you want to be silly while the teacher is talking?

_____

What should you do when you don't understand what the teacher is talking about?

_____

Behaviors for Learning

Page 2 of 2

Can you name any other body or brain behaviors you are supposed to do in school or when your parent, sister, brother, or friend is talking to you?

Hey, I bet you did a good job on this!

But knowing what people expect from you and actually doing all the behaviors right all the time are two totally different things.

Review the list of behaviors for learning listed below. Check which ones are pretty easy for you to do most of the time and which are harder for you to do most of the time. Remember, everybody has trouble with something on the list!

Behaviors	Easy for Me	Harder For Me
Listening with your ears		
Listening with your eyes		
Keeping your feet, legs, hands and fingers calm and quiet		
Sitting where you are supposed to sit		
Keeping your mouth quiet when others are talking		
Thinking about what the teacher is talking about		
Staying focused on the teacher even when another child is silly		

Now, make a plan to help you learn how to take more control over one of the behaviors that is harder for you to do.

Teacher's note: See the handout entitled, "Making a Behavior Plan for Yourself." Also refer to the earlier work in this chapter on changing behaviors through self-awareness, self-monitoring, and self-control.

Helping to Get Ourselves Focused

When my body feels like it has to move, or my brain can't get focused,
I have some strategies to help me to focus.

If my mouth feels like it needs to talk, then I can try to

_____.

If my fingers feel like they need to move, then I can try to

_____.

If my legs feel like they need to move, then I can try to

_____.

If my brain feels like it needs to take a break from thinking, then I can try to

_____.

Try to figure out which of the following strategies would work well for each of the situations above:

- Use a fidget and squeeze it.

- Stand and work by your table rather than sit the whole time.

- Work for two more minutes and then ask to take a 2 minute break.

- Realize that we cannot talk all the time in groups because if we do, the groups can't work well together. (Sometimes it helps to chew on something.)

Trying to Shake a Brain Freeze

A "brain freeze" is when a person's brain gets stuck on a thought or topic. You can work on developing a strategy to try to "thaw out" your brain when this happens. In the thought bubbles below, write down the topics your brain gets stuck.

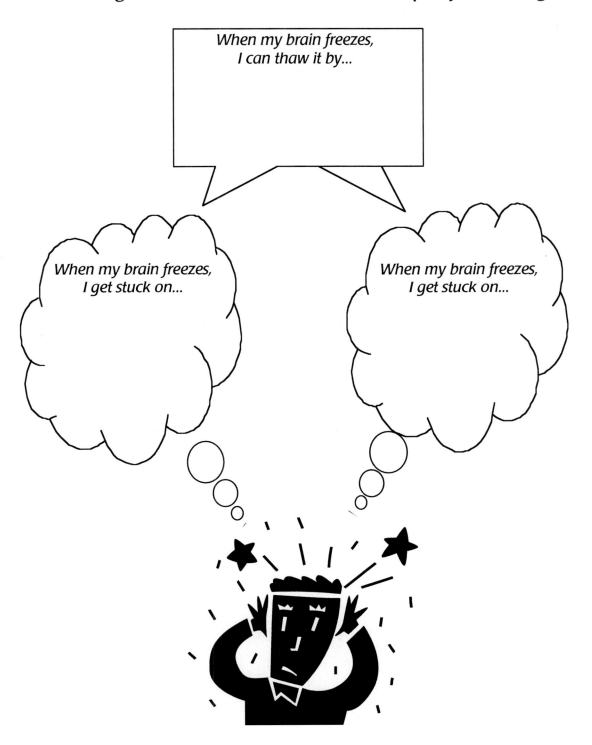

*When my brain freezes,
I can thaw it by...*

*When my brain freezes,
I get stuck on...*

*When my brain freezes,
I get stuck on...*

Perseveration, Perseveration

Perseveration means that you like to talk about the same type of topic over and over again.

Since you like to think about certain things a lot, it is not unusual that you like to talk about certain things a lot.

However, even though other people are interested in you, they like to be able to discuss a variety of topics.

Today we are going to think about what topics you get stuck on and how to work with your brain to convince it that it can get unstuck in order to keep other people wanting to talk to you.

What topic do you get stuck on?

Do you know when you are stuck on the topic?

What are some clues you can look for to help you realize that you are stuck?

How do people respond to you when you are stuck on the topic?

How do people respond to you when you are paying attention to what they like to talk about?

Proud Page

Today you did a bunch of things you should be proud of. Here are some of them!

I am proud of myself because:

Faking It When You Are Not Interested!

The ultimate SOCIAL FAKE is needed to be able to listen to someone talk about something that you are not interested in! When you are in this boring situation, what do you think you can do?

List 3 Choices:

A Bad Choice	*A Good Choice*	*A Good Choice*

What Makes the Bad Choice a Bad Choice?
(Hint: Think about the consequences which will result from each of the choices.)

_____

To do the good choices, what do you have to do with your body and words so that you are really FAKING IT WITH SUCCESS?

_____

What does it mean to "FAKE IT WITH SUCCESS"?

_____

Know Your Boundaries!

Page 1 of 2

What are Boundaries?

1. They are invisible.

2. They mark the lines we should not cross.

3. We can cross people's physical and mental boundaries.a.

    a. PHYSICAL boundaries have to do with where we put our bodies.

    b. MENTAL boundaries have to do with how we make people think and feel about us.

4. If you cross a boundary people may get uncomfprtable and have a weird thought about you.

5. As you get older you can get into serious trouble if you cross a boundary line with your body.

Physical Boundaries:

Let's play some boundary games with our bodies.

I. Discuss and act out the answers to the following questions.
Find the appropriate physical boundary for each situation.

    a. Where can your hands touch other people without that person having a weird thought about you?

    b. How close can your body get to another person?

    c. How long can you stare at another person?

    d. How do you share objects with people without crossing their boundaries? Do you...

        i. ask for people to pass you an object?

        ii. grab what you want?

    e. How are boundaries different if you are with...

        i. your parents

        ii. your teacher

        iii. your friends

        iv. your brother or sister?

Know Your Boundaries!

Page 2 of 2

II. Pretend to throw and catch an imaginary ball. Be aware of each person's body and what he or she is doing with it.

III. Play follow the leader. When the teacher calls "Freeze!" check to see if anyone is crossing someone else's boundary.

IV. Have all the group members line up. Where are the boundaries in line?

V. Play with some blocks. What are the boundary rules for who can touch what blocks?

Mental Boundaries (Thought Boundaries):

Let's play boundary games with our minds. Try these boundary games:

I. One student starts to describe a dog at a park and then the others add something related to what he or she said. Each person needs to consider what the last person said and then add a new part to the story. If you say something related to the last thing that was said, you are staying within your boundaries. But if you say something that has nothing to do with what the group is talking about, you could cross other people's thought boundaries and make them have weird thoughts about what you said. What if someone in the group made a really rude comment about what the group is talking about? What kind of thoughts would that cause others to have?

II. You can figure out what someone else might be thinking about based on what he or she is looking at or touching. Have different students take turns looking at something in the room and then have the rest of the group figure out what he or she is thinking about. If no one paid attention to you when it was your turn, how would you feel? What kind of thoughts would you have?

III. Pick something to talk about and give points to students who talk about the same topic and show that they can stay focused on what other people are thinking and talking about. Pick another topic to talk about and have students make comments which are completely unrelated (i.e. whopping topic changes). Talk about how it feels when no one pays attention to what other people are thinking and talking about.

Hidden Rules in a Barnes and Noble Store

Every place we visit has rules associated with it. However most of the rules are not ones people talk about; they are "hidden rules." Through experience, people start to figure out the rules by watching how other people behave in different situations.

In Barnes and Noble there are many "hidden rules." You will not find a sign in Barnes and Noble Bookstore posting what all the different rules are. You have to figure them out.

The rules have to do with your body, your eyes, your words and your voice level. When you follow the rules, you let people know that you are thinking about them. This is also called "being considerate."

Here is an example of a set of hidden rules within Barnes and Noble Bookstore.

Entering the Building Rules:

> a. Lower the volume of your voice.
>
> b. Hold the door open for the person behind you.
>
> c. Slow down the pace of your walking.
>
> d. If you are with the group, keep your body in the group even if you are interested in a specific section.
>
> e. Tell people in your group where you are interested in looking, or what you want to do.

Hidden Rules in a Barnes and Noble Store

Page 2 of 2

There are many other sets of rules. Figure out what the different sets of rules are for each of the sections below:

1. General book section

2. Kid's section

3. Music Section

4. Magazine Section

5. Big comfy chairs

6. Hanging out in the coffee shop

7. Ordering in the coffee shop

Now that we have considered the rules, we have to learn to monitor our own behavior and the thoughts of others so that we can try to follow the rules to be considerate of others.

Hidden Rules in the School Library

Page 1 of 2

Every place we visit has rules associated with it, however most of the rules are not ones people talk about; they are "hidden rules." Through experience, people start to figure the rules out by watching how other people behave in different situations.

In the school library there are far more than one set of "hidden rules." You will not find a sign in the library posting what all the different rules are. You have to figure them out.

The rules have to do with your body, your eyes, your words and your voice level. When you follow the rules you let people know that you are thinking about them. This is also called "being considerate."

Here is an example of a set of rules for entering the library:

a. Lower the volume of your voice.

b. Hold the door open for the person behind you.

c. Slow down the pace of your walking.

d. If you are with a group, keep your body in the group even if you are interested in a specific section.

e. Tell the people you are with where you are interested in looking or what you want to do.

There are many other sets of rules. Figure out what these different sets of rules are for each of the following:

1. Looking for a book on the shelves

2. Using the computers to locate a book or go on the internet

Hidden Rules in the School Library

Page 2 of 2

3. Asking for help from the librarian

4. Sitting at one of the tables with a group of friends

5. Sitting at one of the tables with people you don't know

6. Checking out books

7. Returning books

Now that we have considered the hidden rules, we have to learn to monitor our own behavior in order to follow the rules. When we do this we are considering other people's thoughts; this is what is meant by being "respectful of others" and "considerate."

If you are not sure of the hidden rules, ask the librarian what is expected in any of the above situations.

Social Judgement

Page 1 of 3

How do you know what people are judging about you?

If you think your behavior is fine, is it really fine? How do you find out?

If you are not sure what is acceptable social behavior, how do you explore what is okay?

What do people judge each other on?

a. _____

b. _____

c. _____

d. _____

Social Judgment involves being aware of the hidden social rules.
Social rules can change from one room to the next, from one event to the next, etc.

What rules change between the classroom and the recess yard?

Why does it matter that you know what the rules are?

Knowing the hidden rules and how these impact people's social judgments is at the heart of social problem solving. You can only realize that you have a problem, or may have a problem, if you realize what the hidden social rules are.

Social Judgment

Here are some potential problems caused at times by people not knowing the hidden rules:

1. sneezing too loud in class

2. talking to yourself while you are around others

3. scratching all parts of your body when they itch

4. telling the teacher she or he is wrong

5. telling other students they don't know what they are talking about in front of the class

6. talking too loud or too soft

7. not talking enough

8. always raising your hand to answer the questions

9. telling people how good your grades are

10. bragging about how much you study

11. talking too much

12. looking at someone for too long

13. standing too close to another person

14. telling people what they should do when you work together in a group

Now consider the "potential problems" above and discuss:

1. If you were the person causing this problem, how would people treat you?

2. What if someone else caused this problem? How would it affect you if you were near this person when he or she caused the problem?

3. How do you monitor your own behavior to avoid being the cause of problems like these?

Social Judgment

Page 3 of 3

4. How do you react to persons who are causing problems so that you don't become a bigger part of the problem? (For example: If someone is standing too close to you and you push the person away, this could result in a fight and you are then considered to be part of a bigger problem.)

If you break the "hidden rules" people think you have weak social skills and they may not be comfortable hanging out with you. We often learn the hidden rules by observing and comparing how people are behaving to how we thought they should behave.

How can you help yourself to figure out the hidden rules around school and at different times at home?

Who can help you figure these out?

Suggestion to the teacher:
Consider having your student(s) document the "hidden rules" to share not only in your group but with other students who will be needing this assistance in coming years. Our students can learn to help themselves as well as others through this effort.

Eat a Turkey - Don't Be One!

Be a "Thinking of You" Person on Thanksgiving

Thanksgiving is coming up and that day is usually filled with lots of food and spending time with family. The holidays are also days when we need to think of others. How can we show others that we are thinking about them on holidays?? Well let's put our brains to work and figure this out!!!!

Why is it important to think about others on Thanksgiving?

_____

How do you want your family and friends to think about you?

_____

What can you do to be a "team player" before the guests arrive?

_____

How can you show Mom (or the person making the food) that you are thinking about her?

_____

What could you say?

_____

How do you show others (cousins, grandparents, aunts/uncles) you are "thinking" about them when they arrive...

    with your body?_____

    with your words?_____

    with your eyes?_____

Eat a Turkey - Don't Be One!

Page 2 of 2

What are 3 things you should remember when talking to a relative?

1. _____

2. _____

3. _____

If you go to someone else's house for Thanksgiving, how do you show those people you are thinking of them when you arrive at their house? What could you say?

_____

_____

How can you show people that you are thinking about others at the table...

with your body?_____

with your words?_____

With your eyes?_____

Give examples of how you can keep making good impressions during the meal.

_____

_____

What is one "thinking of you" thing that you can work on during the day?

_____

Be a Good Problem Solver and Make Good Choices on Thanksgiving

1. What if the turkey is a little burnt and kind of dry? What should you say? What should you not say?

2. What if someone is serving something for dinner that you don't like? What should you say? What should you do? Is this a time to be a flexible thinker?

2. What if you are bored by the conversation at the table?

3. What if you have done a good job being part of the group but you are getting frustrated and you need a break? What can you do?

4. What can you say to your mom and dad ahead of time so that they will be more likely to let you leave the table early?

5. If there are other children at the Thanksgiving party/get-together, what are some ways you could play with them so that they feel you want to be "part of the family?"

Have Yourself a Peaceful Holiday!

Page 1 of 2

Holidays are times when families are supposed to get together and have fun! However, sometimes things don't go so smoothly. Now that you are teenagers, let's figure out how to see the holidays through the eyes of other people in your house:

MOM

- What does Mom WANT the day to be like?
- What stresses Mom out about this day?
- What makes her feel good about this day?
- What does she expect from each of the other people in the house?
- What does she WISH other family members would do on this day?
- If guests are coming, or if your family will be guests at someone else's house, what does Mom want other people in the family to do to help out?

DAD

- What does Dad WANT the day to be like?
- What stresses Dad out about this day?
- What makes him feel good about this day?
- What does he expect from each of the other people in the house?
- What does he WISH other family members would do on this day?
- How does he want other people to help out?

YOU

- What do you WANT the day to be like?
- What stresses you out about this day?
- What makes you feel good about this day?
- What do you expect from each of the other people in the house?
- What do you WISH other family members would do on this day?

Have Yourself a Peaceful Holiday!

Page 2 of 2

Name 3 things you can do differently on this day that would really impress your parents and keep the stress levels of all involved at a minimum?

1. _____

2. _____

3. _____

How much time do you think this will take out of your day?

_____

What will be the benefit of doing these things?

_____

Food for thought: If you do these things there will only be one turkey in the house on Thanksgiving or Christmas!

Taking Time to Give Yourself a Compliment

WE ALL KEEP WORKING ON GETTING BETTER AT THINGS. THIS MEANS WE HAVE TO CATCH OURSELVES WHEN WE ARE NOT DOING SOMETHING WELL, TELL OURSELVES TO DO BETTER, AND THEN WORK AT TRYING TO IMPROVE IT!

As simple as this sounds, it takes a lot of work! It also makes us focus on what is already hard for us, which is usually not fun to do.

SO, WE ALSO NEED TO REMEMBER THAT THERE IS PLENTY THAT WE ALREADY DO WELL, AND WE HAVE TO TELL OURSELVES THAT EACH AND EVERY DAY!

Each day we should make a point to tell ourselves (quietly, in our head…so other's don't think we are boasting) what it is we have done well for that day, hour or moment. The compliments we tell ourselves should focus on small things we have paid attention to and tried to modify. Do not wait until you have done one big thing well to give yourself a compliment. You need to talk to yourself in your positive voice every day!

Go ahead and list 3 little things you have done well today:

1.

2.

3.

When you become good at giving yourself small compliments each day, you are on your way to being your very own coach. The more you can coach yourself, the less you have people telling you what you should do!

Teacher Notes

Section 2

Self Monitoring and Rating Sheets

You Be the Judge!

To observe what is going on socially you need to have a way to think about what you see. Below are some of the things to watch for when you are observing others and determining how they may be observing you.

Part of hanging out with people is watching them to see how they are reacting to you and to figure out what they might be thinking about you or the topic you are discussing.

Rate yourself or someone else on video. There is a lot to observe. You may only want to focus on watching for 2 or 3 areas during one observation period.

Who are you observing? _____ Date _____

Area to Observe	Great	OK	Needs Improvement
Does the person's face look interested in the conversation or activity?			
When the person is talking, does he/she use okay facial expressions? If the person always looks really serious or way too happy, this could be something he/she needs to work on.			
Does the person look with his/her eyes to think about the other person(s)?			
Does the person's body look like he/she wants to stay in the group?			
Does the person use hand and body gestures to help communicate his/her message?			
Is the person initiating comments?			
Is the person initiating questions?			
Does the person only talk about one topic all the time?			
Are the person's comments related to the discussion?			
Does the person respond to other people's questions with enough information?			

Of all the areas reviewed above, what do you think is the most important area for this person to work on? _____

47

Nonverbal Communication Monitor
For Video Moment Review

Your Name: _____

When watching yourself on video, rate yourself using the following guide.

Here are things to look for:	*Put a plus sign (+) each time you see yourself do this well.*
You look with your eyes to watch the person who is speaking.	
Your eye gaze is directed towards the speaker at least 50% of the time.	
Your shoulders are turned in the direction of the group.	
You have an expression on your face that matches the group discussion at least 50% of the time. a. You use eyebrow movement. b. You use a smiley expression. c. You use a sad expression.	
You show interest by leaning in toward the group.	
You show agreement by either nodding or shaking your head.	
Your tone of voice matches the emotions of the discussion.	

Judge for Yourself

Review how the Four Steps of Communication were performed during videotaped interactions.

Name of the person you are observing: _____ Date: _____

Four Steps of Communication:	Describe things that were done well.	Describe things that were a problem.	On a scale from 1 to 5, score the person on how he or she did in each area. 5 is the best score.
1. Thinking about others			
2. Using one's body to show a communicative connection			
3. Using one's eyes to show a communicative connection			
4. Using words to relate to the person he or she is talking to in a positive way so that the listener enjoys what he or she is hearing			

How Am I Doing?

Whatever I learn in this room, I have to think about and try to repeat at home and school and other places.

Today I can watch myself play! I can figure out what I am doing well and I can also figure out things I could do better. When I play today, I am going to figure out how I did.

Nobody is perfect, so I don't expect to do well at everything. My job is to think about how other people are thinking about me!

Fill in the boxes below:

Put a ☺ if you think you did well.

Put a check if you think you did ok.

Put a ☹ if you think you could do a lot better.

Name of the person who is filling out this monitoring sheet: _____

Date and time when the monitoring is done	Keeping my body with the group	Playing a game someone else picks	Following rules that someone else has made up	Listening with my whole body (eyes, hands, ears…)	Monitoring my body's boundaries!

Rating Your Own Interaction on Video

The video will be stopped every minute; rate yourself at that time. Put a tally mark in a box on each row for each rating period. When you are all done with the ratings, you can then count up the tallies and see what you are doing well, what skills are emerging, and what skills you need to continue to develop.

Rate yourself on how you did with the following:	Great, I did this well	Average, it was okay sometimes	OOPS, I didn't do this very well
Asking others questions about themselves			
Commenting about what other people were talking about			
Connecting my comments and questions in to what other people were talking about			
Using my eyes to watch and think about other people when they were talking			
Keeping my head and body turned toward the group			
Talking loud enough so everyone could hear me without struggling to listen or soft enough so that I didn't hurt their ears			

Monitoring Your Thinking About Others Using Video Tape Feedback

Fill in the boxes below:

Put a ☺ if you think you did well.

Put a check if you think you did ok.

Put a ☹ if you think you could do a lot better.

Name of the person who is filling out this monitoring sheet: _____

Actions to Monitor	Rate Yourself	Rate Another Person in the Group
Keeping body turned toward the other person or persons		
Keeping eyes looking toward the other person or persons		
Keeping language focused the other person or persons		

Monitoring Sheet

Name _____ Date _____

The behavior I am monitoring is _____

Each time I do the behavior correctly I will circle an asterisk *
Each time I do it incorrectly, I will cross out an asterisk *

* *

Cut: -

Name _____ Date _____

The behavior I am monitoring is _____

Each time I do the behavior correctly I will circle an asterisk *
Each time I do it incorrectly, I will cross out an asterisk *

* *

Cut: -

Name _____ Date _____

The behavior I am monitoring is _____

Each time I do the behavior correctly I will circle an asterisk *
Each time I do it incorrectly, I will cross out an asterisk *

* * * * * * * * * * * * * * * * * * * *

Think About Social Thinking!

Name _____ Date _____

List of things this person socially adjusted well to when in the classroom:

Social thinking happens during lessons in the school classroom.

Things that were harder to adjust to in the classroom this week:

List of things this person socially adjusted well to when at recess!

Social thinking happens when you are hanging out with others in a fun place!

Things that were harder to adjust to when at recess:

Self Evaluation for Group Assignment

Name:_____ Date:_____

Class:_____

Assignment/Project:_____

Group Members:_____

1. Did I allow others to contribute ideas?	Yes	No
2. Did I listen to group members by staying silent?	Yes	No
3. Did I listen to group members with my eyes and body?	Yes	No
4. Did I encourage others to participate?	Yes	No
5. Did I participate appropriately (not too little, not too much)?	Yes	No
6. Did I do my share of the work (not too little, not too much)?	Yes	No

A strength of mine today was: _____

_____

A weakness of mine today was: _____

_____

Additional comments: _____

_____

_____

Classroom Teacher Mini-Checklist about Social/Organizational Behavior

Dear Teacher,

Your student, _____, is going through an assessment of his/her ability to relate to others and to work as part of a group. It would be very helpful if you could provide the following information based on your own experience with this student.

Please return this form by: _____

Your name: _____

Your relationship to the student: _____

Check the boxes below to indicate how this person is performing in your setting in the following areas:

Skill Areas	Comments	Above Grade Level	At Grade Level	Below Grade Level	Not Observed
Math					
Reading decoding					
Reading comprehension					
Written expression					
Participating as part of the large group during class discussion/lecture					
Participating as part of a small work group in class					
Making and keeping friends during free time					
Ability to ask for help in class					
Organizational skills while in class					
Organizational skills from home to school and back					
Does this child stand out as unique in his/her interpersonal skills either in class or out of class?	Yes or No. If yes, please explain.				
Do you anticipate that this student will encounter more challenges in future school years?	Yes or No. If yes, please explain.				
How would this student's peers describe him/her?					

THANK YOU! Please call me at_____ if you have any questions. Please return this form to:

Name_____   Fax _____

Address_____

Teacher Checklist

Dear Teacher,   Date: _____

_____ is being assessed to determine how he/she functions in the classroom. Please complete the following checklist.

Behavior	Never Happens	Sometimes Happens	Frequently Happens
Raises his/her hand in class			
Participates in a large group during class lectures			
Asks for your help with a specific problem			
Listens to your suggestions and follows them well			
Works successfully with peers as part of a group			
Is observed hanging out with friends outside of class			
Hangs out with friends during free time in class			
Is organized with your class assignments			
Turns in homework on time			
Completes large projects at level of ability similar to his/her classmates			
Comes to you for help outside of class time			

What grade is this student likely to get in your class? _____

Do you feel that this student works up to his/her potential? _____

Comments: _____

_____

Thank you for your help.

Please return the checklist to: _____

___ Please put it in my school mail box   ___ Please fax it to:_____

___ Please mail it to:_____

Paraprofessional Daily Tracking Sheet

Page 1 of 2

Student: _____ Date: _____

Fill out one copy of this form as a prototype and then Xerox it to use on multiple days.

Each day report ONLY on the goal areas which were directly addressed using specific strategies to facilitate learning. Such strategies would involve use of tools such as a checklist, graphic organizer, visual timer, etc.

Indicate if the child did "Well," "OK," or "Not Well."
"Well" = able to follow the strategy and do it with some level of independence
"OK" = able to follow the strategy with a lot of assistance
"Not Well" = resistant or actively refused to work on the strategy

Social Behavioral Functioning
Summarize goals/objectives from the IEP that relate to social understanding.
Fill out a goal line for each new skill being worked on.

	Well	Okay	Not Well
Goal area:			
Goal area:			
Goal area:			
Goal area:			

Comments on social behavioral abilities today: _____

_____

_____

Mark the boxes for the following categories:

Behavior to observe	Participated well	Participated when given assistance	The student stayed by him- or herself.	The student refused to accept assistance
Interacting with peers during recess and free time				
Working as part of the group in class				
Cooperating with class and free time rules				

Academic Functioning

Summarize goals/objectives from the IEP that relate to academic learning.
Fill out a goal line for each new skill being worked on.

	Well	Okay	Not Well
Goal area:			
Goal area:			
Goal area:			
Goal area:			
Goal area:			

Strategy to use during homework time that is being learned at school:

_____

_____

_____

Overall, today was a:

❏ Fine Day - social and school work were good.

❏ Fair Day - some good attempts at social and academic work, but not always successful.

❏ Unproductive Day - poor use of class time to complete academic work even with strategies provided.

❏ Productive with academics but socially it was an unsettled day.

Name of person completing this form: _____

A copy can be sent home to the parent but one copy must stay within the student's file.

Evening Checklist to Use with a Student

Name_____ Date_____

Parents: please use the following marks as you fill out this checklist with your child:

+ = very positive   ✔ = satisfactory   (-) = less than satisfactory
N/A = not addressed today

☐ Did you take your medications?

☐ Did you bring your homework home?

☐ Did you complete all parts of your homework?

☐ Did you ask questions if you did not know what to do for part of your homework?

☐ Did you put all of your work in your binder?

☐ Did you put your binder in your backpack?

☐ Did you put your backpack on the launch pad?

☐ Did you eat your dinner?

☐ Did you stay calm and keep other people feeling calm during dinner?

☐ If you got upset, were you able to control your anger so it did not go on and on and on?

☐ If you started to feel frustrated, did you tell people "I feel frustrated" or "I feel mad" rather than whine and cry?

☐ Did you brush your teeth?

☐ Did you take a bath or shower?

☐ Did you get in bed by 8:30 pm?

☐ Did you go to sleep soon after you went to bed?

Student: How did you do?
Circle a happy face for each "+" or " ✔ " you got on the paper.

☺   ☺   ☺   ☺   ☺   ☺   ☺   ☺   ☺   ☺   ☺   ☺   ☺

The more happy faces circled, the more your parents will tell you how proud of you they are. Getting ready for school can be hard work!

Teacher's Daily Checklist

Name_____   Date_____

- ❑ Arrived at class on time
- ❑ Homework was completed
- ❑ Engaged in positive interactions during small group work
- ❑ Wrote his/her assignments on the assignment-planning sheet
- ❑ Worked productively during class assignments
- ❑ Cooperated as part of a group, adjusting behavior to the needs of others

Please check any behaviors that happened today which were outside of what the group expected:

- ❑ Over-focused on school materials rather than doing his/her school work
- ❑ Walked around the class or did not keep body where it was expected to be
- ❑ Got distracted by other things in the room
- ❑ Disrupted others

Yes / No: The teacher was concerned that the medications were either not given or did not appear to be as effective as usual today (circle one).

The student's mood today was best represented by (circle one):

1. Good, worked as part of the group
2. OK, worked as part of the group much of the time
3. Did not work as part of the group most of the time

Comments: _____

_____

_____

_____

61

Teacher Notes

Section 3

Friendships

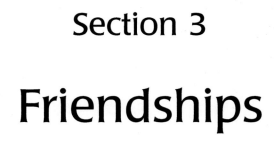

63

How Are Friendships and Interests Related?

Different people have different interests:

Friendships are about being with people you care about and who care about you.
People who are friends do not always share the same interests. But friends show their
friend they are interested in what that person is talking about even when they are not
all that interested in the topic themselves! They do this because they are truly interested
in the person and making that person feel good, even when they may not be totally
interested in everything that person has to say.

Let's think about our own interests and the interests of others.

List two things that are interesting to you.

_____

_____

Now list two things that people in your family are interested in that you ARE NOT interested in.

_____

_____

How do you think people in your family feel when you show you are interested in what
they have to say even though you are not fascinated by the topic they are talking about?

_____

When people have good feelings about us, this usually means we are helping them to
feel good about themselves. How do you feel when people seem interested in what you
have to say? _____

It is likely that when people make you feel good you would describe them as being
"friendly."

Often we talk with other people about our interests. And other people talk with us
about what they are interested in too. Sharing interests is what starts friendships.
Friendships feel good because they help us to feel like we belong and that we have
someone to share our feelings and thoughts with. People we are friends with usually
make us feel pretty good.

Friendships don't just happen; they do take work and patience, but they are worth it!

Having Friends Can Be Hard Work

Getting along with people includes getting along with people at school and at home. It is difficult for each one of us to get along with people all of the time. Sometimes we "get up on the wrong side of the bed." This means we may wake up in a grouchy mood. We are not very friendly when we are grouchy.

Other times we wake up pretty happy. On these days people see us more relaxed and they feel like we are being friendly.

All people have friendly and unfriendly times in their days.

Think about someone you know and describe what he or she looks like when you do not think that person is being friendly. _____
_____

How do you feel when you are around that person when he or she looks like that?
_____
_____

Think about when you have a hard time being friendly. How would people describe what you look like and what you do, when they think you are being "unfriendly"?
_____

How do they feel when they are around you when they think you are being unfriendly?
_____

Even when you feel bad, you can keep working on having people stay with you. Here are some things to try when you are not having a super friendly day.

1. Tell your friends that you do not feel good but you know it is not their fault.

2. Try to focus on what your friends are talking about rather than your own bad feelings. Sometimes other people's good moods can help to change our own grumpy mood to a better mood.

3. Do not spend all your time with your friends complaining about your own bad feelings. Your grumpy mood can make other people feel grumpy.

4. Go for a fast walk, run, or carry something heavy to help your body work out some of its bad energy.

What other things can you think of to do to help you keep playing or working with other people even when your emotions do not feel good?
_____
_____

Getting to Know ME

HELLO MY NAME IS: _____

I AM _____ YEARS OLD

I LIVE IN THE CITY OF: _____

I LIVE IN MY HOUSE WITH: _____
_____

MY FAVORITE HOBBIES ARE: _____
_____

TWO THINGS I REALLY DON'T LIKE TO DO ARE:

1. _____

2. _____

WITH MY FRIENDS I LIKE TO:

1. _____

2. _____

MY FAVORITE GAME TO PLAY OUTSIDE IS: _____

Thanks for doing such a good job! Now people can start to remember some things about you in their "Friend Files."

Once we have a friend,
we keep "Friend Files" in our head...

Page 1 of 2

Friend Files:

As we get to know someone, we learn information about that person through small talk and conversations, and by observing what he or she likes and doesn't like. We store this information in a file in our brain. If we like this person, we say we put this information into our "friend files."

When we see the person again, we open that file and peek inside to remember what we know about him or her. Then we talk about things we know he or she might be interested in. Often we also ask that person questions about what he or she likes to do.

Think about a friend and open your "friend file" for that person. Write three questions you could ask that friend based on what you remember about him or her:

1. _____

2. _____

3. _____

Why do we keep asking someone we already know questions?

When people answer our questions we get even more information to put in our friendly files.

NO ONE is expected to remember everything people tell us. However it is good to remember what you have talked about with people so you don't have the exact same conversation the next time you speak to them.

Using follow-up questions:

When people tell us new information, we can ask questions to find out more about what they are telling us. This is called using "follow-up questions." We ask follow up-questions when we start to wonder what else people know or think about a topic.

Once we have a friend, we keep "Friend Files" in our head…

Page 2 of 2

For example, I see Robyn and I remember from opening my "Robyn file" that she likes to ride horses. So I ask her, "Did you ride any horses this summer?" Robyn says, "I went to horse camp." I can then ask many different follow-up questions. Here are some choices:

1. What was the name of your favorite horse?

2. Do you own a horse?

3. What did you do at the camp?

4. Where was your camp?

5. What was your favorite thing to do with your horse at camp?

Follow-up questions can make the person think you are really interested. You can ask follow-up questions which help bring in things that you might like to talk about related to what the other person is interested in. This can help make the conversation be more interesting to you.

How do you think Robyn feels when people remember things about her and then talk to her about what she likes? _____

_____

How do you feel when this happens to you? _____

_____

Robyn does a good job if she answers with short descriptions to the questions; this means that she does not give too much information because that could be boring to the listeners.

Robyn also does a really good job if, after people ask her some questions, she also remembers what she has in her friend files about them. She can then ask them questions about themselves too.

Try it. Think of a person who is in this group. Remember something that person is interested in. Ask a question about that topic and listen to the answer. Then start to ask him or her some follow-up questions.

Getting good at doing this takes practice!

Different Types of Friends

We all have different types of friends and acquaintances. List some things you do with these different people in the different places.

	Acquaintance	Best Friend	Romantic Boyfriend or Girlfriend
In Classes			
During School Free Time			
At Home or in the Community			

It is expected that we behave in different ways around the same people, depending on what type of place we are in. Each place has a different set of rules which we are supposed to figure out. These rules are called the "hidden rules" since people do not clearly tell you what they are.

How much have you figured out about the "hidden rules?" Who can you ask to learn more about the rules?

Different Types of People...
Different Types of Relationships

Not all people are the same. Some people are good friends of ours. Others we barely know, but they seem nice. And some others may not be nice at all. We have to think about people and try to figure out who is safe and fun to be with. We also need to figure out who we should stay away from!

Different Types of People in our Lives:

FRIENDS	FRIENDLY ACQUAINTANCES	OTHER PEOPLE AROUND YOU WHO SEEM OK (not mean)	OTHER PEOPLE AROUND YOU WHO ARE NOT NICE TO YOU (Mean)
These are people you know and like and choose to spend time with. They do nice things for you and you do nice things for them.	These are people you don't know very well, but they seem to be nice to you.	These folks are fine; just keep an eye on them!	These people are dangerous; they may try to trick you in a bad way.
What do you do with friends?	What do you do with friendly acquaintances?	What do you do around people you don't know?	What do you do around people that you KNOW are often mean to you?

The Nasty Side of Social Behavior... Coping with Jerks!

Page 1 of 2

Even though you have explored thinking about and modifying your own social behavior so that people have reasonably good thoughts about you, there are still plenty of people out there who are JERKS!

Jerks seem to feel good at the moment they make other people feel bad.

Some jerks are more likely to be jerks when they are with their jerky friends. Other jerks are jerks even when they are by themselves since they seem to think that making other people feel bad gives them a lot of control.

Some jerks are actually good people who do not always act "good." All good people are at risk for being a jerk at one time or another. You are always encouraged to make sure that you don't act like a jerk in the eyes of other people.

However, you cannot control the jerk factor in most other people. But even though you cannot control it, you do need to know when you are the victim of a jerk.

Victims are people that fall into the jerk's trap. When this happens, it is not your fault, but you do need to be aware of what you are dealing with so that you can get out of the trap as soon as possible! This can be confusing though because jerks can put you in some really bad situations that make the victims feel like they are at fault.

Defenders are people who get out of the jerk's trap or avoid the trap all together. Defenders are people who end up being able to get rid of the jerk or avoid being "jerked around" when jerks are near.

Aggressors are people that try so hard to avoid being "jerked around" that they end up becoming jerks themselves. Aggressors come on very strong and make people wonder if they are trying to control things. Aggressors do not take advice well from other people.

The Nasty Side of Social Behavior...
Coping with Jerks!

Page 2 of 2

Explore each type of reaction, Victim, Defender, and Aggressor, in each of the following situations:

1. Working in a small group in class

2. Hanging out by your self during lunch time at school

3. Being alone or in close quarters with a person of the opposite sex

4. Being with your siblings

Victims	List some warning signs that you are becoming a victim.	List some things you can do once you realize you are a victim.
Defenders	List some signs that you have been a good defender.	List some things that defenders do to take care of themselves.
Aggressors	List some signs that you are acting like an aggressor.	List some things you can do to bring yourself back to a calm level.

In the eyes of others... you are who you hang out with!

When you hang out by yourself, people focus on you. People might concentrate on how you look, what you do, what you say, and what your personality is like.

When you hang out in a group of kids, people focus on the group rather than on the specific people in it. They consider how the group looks, what the people in the group do, and what they say. Sometimes people behave differently in a group than they would by themselves.

What type of impression do people get from the group that you hang out in? Describe your group according to how it looks, what you do in the group, and what people in your group might talk about.

_____
_____
_____
_____

Impressions can be good, bad, or so-so. How do impressions about your group rub off on you when you are not in the group?

_____
_____
_____
_____

If you want to make a better impression than your group made on someone specific, what are some things you can think about and do around that person?

_____
_____
_____
_____

Friends are a great thing...
until people get too wild!

Think about this scenario. You have friends over to your house and they start to act crazy by saying or doing bad things. When your friends are like this it rubs off on you and you start to act wild too.

When this happens, what is the point of view of the following people?

You	Your Friends	Your Parents

How do you deal with it all?

Who is in charge of the friends when your friends come to your house?

_____

List two things you could do when they first come over:

1. _____

2. _____

List two things you could do once they start to get wild:

1. _____

2. _____

If it has been crazy, what do you need to do once your friends leave?

_____

_____

How does the behavior of you and your friends affect your parents' point of view?

_____

_____

_____

Keeping and Losing Friends

Things to do to keep friends:

1. Be pretty truthful.

2. Be trusting.

3. Listen to friends when they need you to; sometimes hold your own thoughts.

4. Know how you are to act with friends in different places.

5. Talk about things other people like even if you don't love the topic.

6. Call or instant message people.

7. Ask people to do things on weekends or after school.

8. Look interested in them when you are with them.

Things to do to lose friends:

1. Be two faced.

2. Tell them everything you think (For example, tell people if you think they are fat).

3. Be rude.

4. Talk trash about people that your friends like.

5. Talk too much about the same topic.

6. Look or act like you are not interested.

7. Insist that your decisions are the most important.

8. Join a group that you are not invited into (crash it).

Good Players

Good players are people who play well or work well with other people. All people like it when other people work well with them.

Good players don't just play on the playground. They also work well with other people at home, in the classroom during activity time, and even while waiting their turns at their desks. Good players also include those who wait in line well.

When we come to this social thinking group, we are learning to be better players.

Here Are the Rules for Being a Good Player:

1. Move your body to stay with the group. Sometimes these are big movements like walking across the playground, and other times they are small movements that just involve moving your shoulders to stay with the group.

2. Think with your eyes. Stay alert and watch what people are doing, what they might be feeling, and where they might be looking!

3. Think about the people you are with. What do they want from you? How are they feeling when they are playing in your group? How close should your body be to them?

4. If it's a little boring for you but fun for the others, stay with the group...
because you know that when it is fun for you it might be a little boring for them.

5. Know that no one knows it all! Being a good player means not telling people everything you know. People want to play with you not just to learn from you! Sometimes people actually get mad if someone always tries to tell them things. They feel like the person is acting like a "know it all." Being a "know it all" is not a friendly thing to do. Other people like to feel that they also know special things.

All people keep learning to be better players!

Being a good player takes a lot of thinking, play, and practice to get it right!

We are so proud of you for how hard you are trying!

 © Michelle Garcia Winner 2005 • www.socialthinking.com

Some Rules of Friendship

We are having fun learning about how to be good friends this week. We are playing games together, sharing toys, making snacks for each other, and thinking about each other.

When we think about our friends and how they feel, that helps everyone to have a good time together. Here are some rules that help us think about and do what other people expect from us:

1. **People expect us not to get too close to them when talking together or standing in line.** They expect us to stand about one arm's length away from other people.This is called THE ONE ARM RULE. Practice the "one-arm rule."

2. **People expect other people to be nice.** Saying words that make everyone feel good helps people to LIKE YOU! Be nice to others.

3. **People expect people to stick together when they are in a group.** Walking away from the group makes people feel like you don't want to be with them. Keep your body with the group.

4. **All people like to go first, but only one really can.** People expect other people to understand that everyone has to take a turn at being first. Even if the other students don't make a big deal about it, they still like being able to go first! Don't get upset when you don't get to go first.

5. **All people like to win, but only one person or one team can.** People expect other people to still act like a nice friend even when they lose. All people on earth have times they win and times they lose. All people like to win, but they realize that this is not possible or even fair to all the other people. When you don't win a game, say something friendly to the winner.

When we follow these rules, everyone has a better chance of having friends.

When we don't follow the rules, then we should take time to think about the rules and why they are important.

Sitting in the "think chair" gives you time to remember why the rules are important.

Friendships Can Be Messy at Times!

People are complicated! They have thoughts, feelings, different experiences, different beliefs, and different purposes for acting the way they do. Just because we like someone doesn't mean that it is easy to get along with that person all the time.

However, when we are aware of what makes people feel good or bad, it is easier to adjust our own behavior so that the other people don't feel bad even when we are having a bad day.

Let's think about how to mess up a friendship and how to try and keep a friendship clean!

Top 10 Ways to Mess Up a Friendship	Top 10 Ways to Keep a Friendship Clean
1.	1.
2.	2.
3.	3.
4.	4.
5.	5.
6.	6.
7.	7.
8.	8.
9.	9.
10.	10.

Messing up a friendship can cause some problems. Then you have to try some problem solving strategies. What are some strategies that have worked for you?

Enjoying Other People

Draw a picture of things you like to think about doing with other people!

Section 4

Being Part of
a Group

Doing Things as a Group

There is a difference between being near a group doing only what you want (being a "Just Me" person) and learning to work with other people to create something together (being a "Thinking about You" person).

What are things you would do if you were a "Thinking of You" person in the group?	What would you do if you were a "Just Me" person in the group?
Think about the people who are in the group.	Think about what you want to be able to do in the group.
Keep your body with the group.	Go where ever you want in the room.
Think with your eyes to consider the other people's plans, emotions, etc.	Look at things in the room rather than at the people you are with.
Use part of your body or face to communicate.	Just have a blank stare when people talk to you.
Balance every instruction you give someone with a compliment for that person.	Tell people what to do all the time since you are smart and you know what everyone should do!
If you are not sure what to say, tell people what you are doing. When they tell you what they are doing, pay attention by looking at them or making a simple supportive comment like "Cool."	Stay quiet the whole time since you like to keep your thoughts to yourself. or… Just tell people what you like to think about all the time.

83

Social Thinking in Social Groups

What to Do When People Start Talking

1. Figure out what they are really trying to tell you. What is the topic?

You may have to listen for a while to figure out what people are really talking about. *Tip: It is a good idea to enter into a group quietly and thoughtfully and allow yourself time to observe and think about what other people are doing and saying.*

2. Wonder and think about what you can ask to find out more about the topic, and then ask them the question.

But stay alert; sometimes threads of topics change quickly and by the time you have the chance to ask your question, the discussion may have moved onto something else. *Tip: Asking someone a question makes the other person feel like they are smart and helpful!*

3. Think about how what is being talked about connects to your own life experience. Share that thought with the others in the group.

For example, if you are telling me about what your dog did wrong over the weekend, it can make me think about my dog and what she does that is silly. I can then share that story. *Tip: Adding experiences to what other people are talking about shows you are interested in the discussion and that you have interesting things in your life as well.*

4. When other people add their thoughts, show you are interested by keeping your eyes and body focused on the person in the group who is speaking.

Tip: All people in the group have thoughts about what the others are doing (with their body positions, their eyes, etc.) Even when people are talking, they have thoughts about the other people who are around them. While you may be silent in a group, your presence is not at all "invisible."

5. When it is your turn to talk, talk for no more than 15-30 seconds at a time.

If people are interested in what you have to say, they will ask questions or make comments about your topic. *Tip: Even if you have much more knowledge and much more to say, limit how long you speak. This allows others a turn to talk. If you go on and on about your topic people may feel you are not letting them speak. "Too much information" may not be interesting to others even if it is interesting to you.*

General Rules for Social Thinking Groups

Our social thinking group is a lot like school. There is a teacher and there are students.

The teacher has a lesson to teach and the students are together to learn something.

However, the social thinking group is not like school in that once the lesson is taught, the students get to do activities to practice different parts of the lesson. The teacher has planned something fun for you to do, but it is important that we work together as a group or the plans may fall apart.

Here are some rules for working together as a group here:

1. Pay attention with your eyes to what the teacher or the other students are talking about.

2. Pay attention with your ears to what other people are saying. Make guesses. What does this mean you are supposed to do?

3. Keep your body calm by using fidgets and thinking about the other people in the group. Ask yourself, "What do they expect from me??"

4. Only say things that have to do with what the whole group is working on, and only say something that ADDS to the group's discussion.

Comments that students make that do NOT ADD to the group are called "blurts".

Blurts can be:

a. Comments that talk about someone else's not so good behavior

b. Comments that provide extra detail that no one asked for
   (Because many of us already are making "guesses" in our heads when other people are talking, we don't need all the details said out loud. We have already guessed them in our head.)

c. Comments that interrupt the teacher or other students
   (These can make people forget the most important part of what they were trying to say.)

d. Comments that make people laugh when it is not a "let's be funny time"

e. Comments that even agree with the teacher if they are always made out loud

(People keep many thoughts in their heads and don't let them out of their mouths!!)

Being Part of a Group

Page 1 of 2

When you are part of a group of people you need to think about whether or not the things you say are important to all of the people who are there.

Information that is being shared is good information if it relates to the topic of the group and if it has not already been said before. That means you have to listen to all of the other people's thoughts and only share NEW information.

There are times when a whole group feels strongly that they want to do something one way and you may feel strongly that you want to do it another way. What do you do at that point? Should you continue to talk about what you want, or should you be flexible and do what the larger group is suggesting (as long as this is not an unsafe decision).

Sometimes you really do want to disagree with the whole group. Be aware that this is likely to make some people impatient and even frustrated. But if you believe that what you have to say is really important, you need to respect the fact that other people think that their idea is just as good as yours.

Spoken information that is not important to other members of the group can irritate people because they feel it wastes their time.

Being Part of a Group

Page 2 of 2

Here are some examples of information that other people don't need to know:

• Why you personally can't attend a meeting set for a specific time. All they need to know is if you can or cannot come. They do not need to know why.

• What your personal problems were that came up during the day.

• That people should do it your way just because you want them to.

Can you think of more examples?

_____

_____

_____

How much time should you talk in a group?
You need to consider the size of the group to answer this question.

Be aware that the larger the group, the less time each person in the group should speak. If there are two people in a group, each person should speak about 50% of the time.

When there are four people in the group, each person should speak about 25% of the time.

When there are 30 people in the group, not all 30 people are going to actually talk. Those that do talk should be very aware that they are taking up the time of 29 other people. Therefore they should probably not talk more than 10% of the total time.

87

Social Thinking in a Group

Name_____   Date_____

To be part of a group you have to think socially. This means you have to think about the other people in the group. It is really easy to get caught up in thinking about your own feelings (especially when you are meeting new people). But let's work on thinking about the other people who are here.

1. Write down what you think about the other people in the group.

   a. Does everyone seem comfortable? Do people seem happy to be here?

   b. Has anyone done something to make you feel badly? If so, what?

   c. Has anyone done something to make you feel good? If so, what?

   d. What do you think some of the other people are thinking about you?

2. You can tell how some of the people feel by looking at their faces as well as their posture and body language.

   a. How do you know who feels good?

   b. How do you know who might feel nervous or who doesn't want to be here?

3. What do you want to ask some people to find out about them?

   a. Write down a question you can ask another student in the room.

   b. Write down what you would like to ask your teacher about this group or what you are working on as part of the group.

4. Write down why your parent is bringing you here.

5. Write down what you would like to do this year with this group.

Our Ideas on How to Be Together As a Group

Each social group that comes together at school has some unwritten rules about different aspects of the group. As a social thinking group, discuss what some of your group's "unwritten rules" are with regards to the following areas. Have one person keep track of the information.

Clothing: Most students dress "appropriately." What would be some examples of clothes that a person might wear that would make the group have "weird thoughts?"

Rules: Each group has some rules. Most of these rules are pretty familiar (e.g. Be nice. Allow other people to talk.) Are their any special "unwritten rules" in this group?

Discussion: What are common topics of discussion which have been accepted by this group? What would be a topic of discussion that would make people feel uncomfortable?

Media: The media (internet, TV, movies, music) is a common part of people's lives. Are there certain TV shows, movies or music stations that kids in this group should pay attention to?

Staying in contact: A really important aspect of a social group is finding time to talk to each other even when the group is not meeting at its regular time and place. What is the preferred type of contact for this group? Cell phones? Instant messaging? Telephones?

Where you could go together: A big part of a being in a group is sharing experiences with the members of the group that you do not get to have with other people at home or at school. What types of activities would this group like to do together?

Rules We Can Live By

The following rules were written by a group of 3rd graders. Can your group develop your own rules if all the adults' rules are removed from the group?

Rules for our bodies:

1. Stop means stop
2. Don't fight!
3. Don't hit!
4. At the table, raise your hand when you want to talk.
5. If you want a drink or to go to the bathroom, ask!
6. Water is only for drinking.
7. No crying or screaming unless someone is really hurt!
8. Walk in the halls quietly!
9. Have at least one wiggle break per session.

Rules for thinking about others:

1. Share the toys.
2. Play fairly and by the rules.
3. Stay with the group and do what the group is doing.
4. When someone is talking, don't interrupt.
5. Don't make a big deal out of colors. Being with people is more important than the color of the chair you are sitting in!
6. You have to pay attention to the person speaking.
7. Listen with your eyes!
8. Take turns talking.
9. Don't hog the toys.
10. Talk to people about what they want to talk about!
11. Don't hog the talk!

I can try to follow the rules. Some days will be better than others, but if I show that I am trying then I know that other people will enjoy being with me!

If I have a really, really bad day and I scream or hit or run away from the group, then my teacher will ask me to sit in a chair to quietly calm down. If I don't stay in the chair, I MUST leave the room to calm down because otherwise the group can't concentrate on being together. I can come back in the room when I am ready to work with the rest of the group and follow the rules above. Everyone likes me to be in the group with them! They don't like it when I have to leave the group.

Being with a Group Is a Privilege

Learning as part of a group at school takes some extra effort from everyone! The teacher has to work hard to make sure every one understands what she's teaching.

All students have to work on focusing on their behaviors for learning.

When a student is not able to learn as part of the group during a lesson, it can be harder for the whole group to learn. One student who can't concentrate causes other students to have a hard time focusing on what they need to do. This may even make it hard for the teacher to continue teaching.

When this happens, the teacher may feel it is important for that student to leave the group so that everyone else can continue.

If that student is you, your job now is to:

1. Calm down – Sometimes this may mean you should go to your quiet place to get your brain and body working together better.

2. Review with a teacher or other adult the behaviors for learning you are concentrating on, plus any other behaviors that happen to be not-so-good at that time. Remember that other people have thoughts about how each person in a group participates.

3. Set a small goal for yourself to refocus on your behaviors for learning.
   Write your goal down.
   _____

4. Practice using your behaviors for learning by doing some of your class work in a quiet place, by yourself.

5. If it worked and you could get your brain and body focused to learn, talk to the adult you are with to see if she or he agrees that you are ready to go back to class!

   You can say, "I think I got my brain and body working together better. I think I am ready to go back to class. What do you think?"

6. Now it's time to remember your classroom "behaviors for learning" goals and go be part of the group!

Group Work, Group Rules

When we are with groups, some of the time we are interested in what is going on, and at other times we aren't really interested in what is being said or done. At the times we aren't interested, we have to fake it and like we are interested. Why do we have to fake it? _____

List 3 ways in which you can fake it (be serious!)

1. _____

2. _____

3. _____

How many people does it take to destroy a group? _____

In this class, each parent/teacher feels the students will benefit from a group experience to learn about how to talk to, think about, and relate to other people...as well as learn better problem solving skills.

Like any group, this group falls apart as soon as one person goofs off, or one person insists on talking the whole time. Once this group falls apart, no one benefits from being in the group.

Here are some rules to follow so that we can all benefit from the group:

1. We only say comments that respect each person, and make each person feel good about being in our presence.

2. We follow the leader of the group, whether that is a student or teacher, without question or rude comment.

3. We refrain from interruptions, unless they are totally related to the topic at hand.

3 Strikes Policy: (Which is not open for debate!)

I assume that all students who come to this group have a great deal of awareness about their behavior and how to think about others in the group...since we have spoken about this for months. It is now time to set a clear expectation. Simply, I expect you to be able to work to follow the three rules above. If you can not do them one day then we have a "3 strikes and you're out for 5 minutes" policy. You will get up to 3 warnings (which is really generous!) and then you will have to leave the room or sit in the corner of the room.

Being part of a group is always a privilege; let's work to continue to recognize that!

Group Rules for When Things Go Sour

Rules for being part of ANY group:

1. Pay attention to the group; this means listen to what is being said and look at the face of the speaker and/or others nearby who are also in the group.

2. Keep your body in the group, with shoulders facing the group.

3. Add your thoughts, comments and questions to the group!

Rules for being part of a group WHEN THINGS DON'T TURN OUT THE WAY YOU WANT!

When things don't turn out the way we want, we all feel any number of emotions which might include feeling frustrated, annoyed, angry, mad, sad, disappointed, stressed, furious, etc.

Even when we feel one of these ways, other members of the group still expect certain behaviors from us.

Behaviors that are EXPECTED even if you are upset include:

1. Sad face

2. Words of disappointment like "darn" or "shoot"

3. A steady voice that is not loud

4. You may get a chance to explain why you feel upset. At other times there is no need to explain; it is just what you have to put up with. For example, if someone else gets to go first, you do not need to explain why you are upset. However, if you lose your favorite pen, you may need to explain this because no one knows why you are sad.

Group Rules for When Things Go Sour

Page 2 of 2

When you do expected behaviors even when you are sad or upset, other people stay calm and are more willing to help you.

Here are behaviors that are UNEXPECTED even if you are upset:

1. Angry face
2. Yelling out your thoughts about why you are mad
3. Telling people how much you hate them
4. Big gestures showing people that your body is going out of control
5. Running away or hiding
6. Refusing to do any more work
7. Insisting things have to go your way
8. Hitting
9. Saying bad words

When you do these unexpected behaviors it makes other people feel angry or sad themselves. When they feel this way it is hard for them to treat you well during that time.

We know things are not going to go well every day, so each day we get to practice trying to keep our behaviors doing what others expect so other people can continue to work with us and help us.

Being First and Taking Turns

Sometimes when I am with my friends we play games and share toys. When we play, it is fun to take turns being first. My friends and I can each have turns being first. I can be first sometimes, and I can let other people go first at other times. I can feel good when I let other people go first because I know it makes them feel good.

It is important to take turns so that everyone can have fun. I can work on taking turns being first. When we play together, I can let my friends be first sometimes.

Here is a picture of me letting someone else be first.

95

Playing a Game When You Are in a Group

Even when you are playing, you still have to think about the other people in the group. Always think about the people you are playing with!

Here are some things to think about:

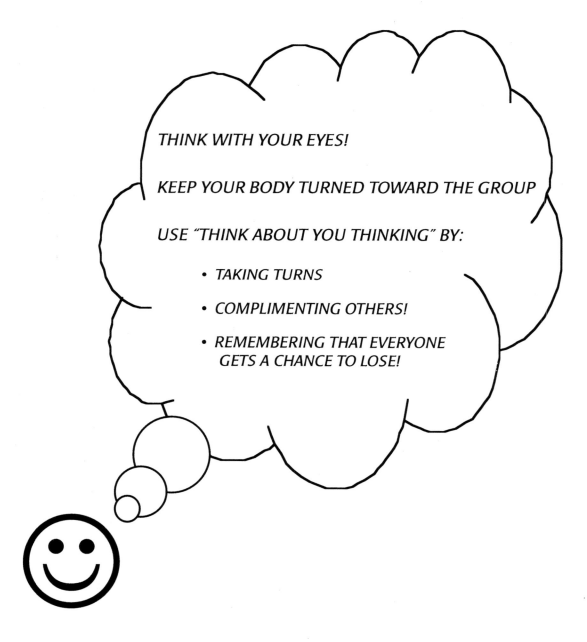

THINK WITH YOUR EYES!

KEEP YOUR BODY TURNED TOWARD THE GROUP

USE "THINK ABOUT YOU THINKING" BY:

- TAKING TURNS

- COMPLIMENTING OTHERS!

- REMEMBERING THAT EVERYONE GETS A CHANCE TO LOSE!

Cooperation and Competition

Cooperation and competition take a lot of practice, but you can feel really good when you get it right!

Of course you want to…
- Be the one to win
- Always go first
- Never get bored

We all want that…but we can't have it and be with other people too!

WHY NOT? _____

_____

Being with other people means:
It feels good to laugh with someone else
It feels good to play with someone else
It feels good to talk to someone else

Being with other people also means:
Each person wants a chance to go first
Each person wants a chance to win
Each person wants a chance to talk and be listened to

This means that sometimes you have to think more about how good the other person feels, than how bad you think you feel.

That means that sometimes you have to do what someone else enjoys,
even if it is not your favorite thing!

97

Cooperation and Competition

And that means that sometimes you have to talk to people about something you don't love to talk about…

Because being with other people and helping them want to be with you is one of the most important things you can do!

Draw a picture of playing a game with a friend.

Section 5

Exploring
Language Concepts

Indirect Language:
What does it really mean?

Teachers, parents and friends say things that imply what they mean, but they often don't say exactly what they mean. Curiously, women are more indirect with language than men. It is important to note that when people use very direct language, it is often interpreted that they are angry!

101

Indirect Language

Below is a chart we are creating to help us think of different indirect expressions and then decipher their real meaning

Indirect language or humor:	Direct, literal meaning of the words:
"Listen up."	"Be quiet now!" or "Shut up!"
"I'll take care of that."	"Don't touch it." or "I want to do it."
"Thank you" (as a response to an answer you have provided in class)	"Your turn is done. Do not keep talking."
"Time to work."	"Get out your materials, get your body into your chair and don't talk to others."
"This is a good time to turn it in."	"Turn it in now."
"Knock it off."	"Stop whatever you are doing that is making someone frustrated."
"It would be great if you guys discussed this topic."	"Stop talking about other things and stay on task."
"It would be nice if you got your binder organized."	"It's time to do it now, and don't do anything else."
"Why don't you guys work on your own?"	"Stop talking and looking at each others' papers."
"We have a test to study for," (as you approach a group)	"You are not welcome in this group."
"If you have a moment, why don't you set the table?" (at home)	"Set the table now."
"I am really busy."	"I don't have time to talk to you."
"You guys are really bothering me."	"Change your behavior."
"I am not having a good day." or "Life sucks."	"Be nice to me."
"In a minute." or "Just a second."	"Not right now. I need some time to finish up my thought or what I am doing."
"You are such a loser," or "You're a retard," or "I hate you!" etc...	Some indirect expressions are forms of sarcasm and you can only tell what they mean based on how close you are to the person saying them. If the person is a close friend, then each of these expressions could be expressions of admiration. But if you don't know the person well, then he or she might say one of these expressions with a smile but possibly really mean it!
Can you think of some more?	

Interpreting Indirect Questions

Page 1 of 2

Indirect questions are questions people ask you because they want to find out some information from you without bluntly asking it.

For some reason, as our society has evolved we have determined that polite people don't often make direct requests of others.

Your job as the receiver of these questions is to figure out what the MOTIVE or INTENTION of the person asking the question is. You have to ask yourself what this person really wants from you. What is the person planning to do with the information you have given him or her?

Indirect questions are a very normal part of our lives. We must be prepared to handle them so that people do not get angry at us or take advantage of us. Once you figure out people's intentions, you can better determine how you want to handle the situation. You do not have to give people what they want, but you have to politely get yourself out of the situation. Being BLUNT is not considered "polite."

In the following table, look at each scenario and the associated indirect question. Your job is to figure out what the person really wants from you and contrast that with what the question literally means. I have given you an example to get you started.

Scenario and Indirect Question	What does the person asking the question really want from you? How should you respond?	If you interpreted the question literally, how would you respond?
Example: You are in the lunch line at school and a friend says to you, "Hey, do you have any money?"	Their intention: They want me to pay for their lunch. So I can say, "No, I told my mom I would give her back the change."	I would probably tell the person how much money I really have.
Try to solve this: You are in class and a fellow student says to you, "I forgot about my homework last night. Can I see yours?"		

Interpreting Indirect Questions

Page 2 of 2

Scenario and Indirect Question	What does the person asking the question really want from you? How should you respond?	If you interpreted the question literally, how would you respond?
Try to solve this: You drove your car to school and an acquaintance says, "I forgot to tell my sister to come pick me up today. What are you doing after school?"		
Try to solve this: You are out at the mall with some acquaintances. One asks, "Hey, how much money do you have?" as he/she show you something he/she wants to buy.		
Try to solve this: Your teacher is in a bad mood and says, "Who wants to get me upset today?"		
Try to solve this: You go turn on your computer games and your mother walks in and says, "Is your room clean?"		

Working on Making Smart Guesses

Name _____ Date _____

Use this while playing "20 Questions!"

List each fact learned in a circle. Combine all the information in the circles to make a smart guess about the answer. All "good guesses" consider ALL the information in each of the circles.

A Good Guess is:

Making Guesses…

The big word is "Inferencing"

Inferencing involves making a smart guess based on information that you have already learned. Sometimes we learn information through reading and talking; other times we learn information by watching what is happening around us. We can guess what is going to happen next in a class by learning the class routines. We can also watch what the teacher is doing and get clues as to what she or he is planning to do next. We figure out what people expect from us by watching their reactions.

What can you "infer" in the following situations?

1. The teacher picks up your class' math book:

_____

_____

_____

2. Your friends are trying to study and you keep talking. They keep rolling their eyes when you talk:

_____

_____

_____

3. Your mom looks really upset because she came home and saw you were still on the computer and your school books were not on the table:

_____

_____

_____

Words to Know, Use and Think About

Name _____ Date _____

1. Logical

2. Illogical

3. Relevant

4. Irrelevant

5. Inference

6. Consequence

7. Making an Impression

8. Initiating

9. Forming a Perspective

More information on these concepts is in the book *Transfer Activities: Thinking Skill Vocabulary Development*, Mayo, P. and Gajewski, N. (1987) Thinking Publications. www.thinkingpublications.com

Getting from **Details** to **Main Ideas** or **Concepts**

Details are facts.

They are often things you can touch, feel and see. Details may include what things look like, location, what people are doing, and even how they feel. Details are usually things we can list.

For example the details you notice in a room might include:

1. There are two people.

2. They are sitting at a table talking to each other.

3. There is a clock on the wall that says 11:24 am.

4. There is a red box on the book shelf.

4. There are papers on the table.

5. The people look like they are concentrating on the papers and what each other is saying about the papers.

Concepts are ideas.

Concepts are what you understand AFTER you have considered how the details go together. For example, we can use the above set of details to make some "smart guesses" or "educated guesses" about what is going on in that setting. We can do this because we have had a lot of experiences in our life. We know that when we see certain sets of details together, we can then understand what is happening based on our past experiences.

What MAIN IDEA or CONCEPT do you have about what the details above mean since they are clustered together?

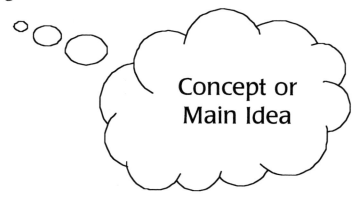

Concept or Main Idea

Getting from **Details** to
Main Ideas or **Concepts**

Too many details… Not all of them are important.

Since details are the key to figuring out the Concept or Main Idea, the TRICK is to figure out which ones are important and which ones are just TMI (TOO MUCH INFORMATION). Our brain has to act as a filter to determine which details we need to focus on.

THE MOST CRITICAL DETAIL THAT HAS TO BE CONSIDERED IS WHAT PEOPLE ARE FEELING IN THE SETTING. Thus, always consider:

1. Emotions of the characters

2. The setting (Tears on a person's face likely mean sadness in a funeral parlor; tears at a wedding are probably tears of joy.)

3. Whether people are paying attention to each other or ignoring each other

4. What details help you to define what the characters are doing in the setting? For example: in the set of details on the previous page, the papers help us to know the people are working, and not eating, at a table.

Which details listed on the previous page ARE NOT necessary for figuring out the CONCEPT or MAIN IDEA? Cross out the details that do NOT help you to get to the Main Idea or Concept.

The truth is that we have to figure out the Main Idea or Concept each time we approach a new situation. This is true whether the situations appear in real life (like when you walk into a room of people and have to figure out what is going on), are seen in pictures, or are read in passages in books.

How do you do this same type of thinking when you are:

1. In an airport?

2. In the lunchroom at school?

3. In your math class?

4. Reading your English book?

5. Writing a paper?

6. Looking at someone's vacation pictures?

Getting from **Details** to **Main Ideas** or **Concepts**

Sorting out Details to Get to the Main Idea

Read a passage assigned by your teacher. Write down the DETAILS that you THINK help you to figure out the CONCEPT or MAIN IDEA. We call these the RELEVANT DETAILS.

Relevant Details
1.
2.
3.
4.
5.

Write down some of the details that DO NOT help you to get to the MAIN IDEA or CONCEPT; these are called IRRELEVANT DETAILS.

Irrelevant Details
1.
2.
3.
4.
5.

NOW, Consider the RELEVANT DETAILS and make an EDUCATED GUESS based on your own experiences about what the MAIN IDEA or CONCEPT is in this passage.

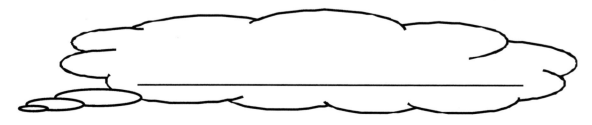

Words Are Not As Simple As They Appear

Behavioral Concepts

Some words are easy to understand because they just label objects. Describe what you see in your head when you think about each of those words.

Tree   Chair   House   Dog

Some words are complicated because they talk about CONCEPTS. Some "concepts" actually describe a set of ideas. It is much more difficult to describe a concept because it is not something that you can touch or see.

"Behavioral concepts" relate to a set of behaviors we are supposed to use when in the presence of others. However, a behavioral concept does not clearly list exactly the behaviors that one is supposed to do; instead we are supposed to figure out what each concept means and from there, determine which behaviors to do.

Look at the following words. Think about these behavioral concepts and write down 4 behaviors that go with each one:

Cooperate

1.

2.

3.

4.

Participate

1.

2.

3.

4.

Respect

1.

2.

3.

4.

Interact

1.

2.

3.

4.

These behavioral concepts are pretty complicated to define, yet we are all expected to understand the general idea of each one. In fact, people form impressions of us based on how they see us respond in situations that demand these behavioral concepts.

If you are not sure what one of these means, discuss it as a group.

Words for Thinking about What People Think

We want to make sure that students are very familiar with these types of words and can use them to talk about other people's thoughts and knowledge accurately. We need students to understand the contents of people's minds to some extent before we assume they can learn to adjust to the unstated expectations of others.

Think

Know

Guess

Remember

Forget

Decide

Teacher Notes

Section 6

Developing Effective Communication

115

The Four Steps of Communication

1. Thinking about people and what they think and feel

    a. Ask yourself, "What are the people near me interested in?"

    b. How do they feel about what you are saying?

    c. What are you doing to show you are interested in them when they are talking?

2. Being aware of your physical presence as well as the physical presence of others

    a. Your body position shows who you want to talk to (or who you do not want to talk to).

    b. Your body movements show what you plan to do next. This communicates messages to people, even if you are not trying to communicate.

    c. Your body language and facial expression communicate how you feel about things and people around you.

3. Using your eyes to think about others and see what they are thinking about

    a. The direction of people's eyes lets others see what they might be thinking about.

    b. We use our eyes to help figure out how other people feel, what they are thinking about, and if they are interested in the other people they are with.

4. Using your language to relate to others

    a. Talk about things that are interesting to others.

    b. Ask questions to find out about people; make comments to show interest.

    c. Add your own thoughts to connect your experiences to other people's experiences.

    d. Adjust your language to what the group or other person is talking about.

Considering How the Four Steps of Communication Impact this Group

Name _____ Date _____

Developing your own awareness of yourself and others around you is a big, big part of "hanging out."

Four Steps of Communication	What have I done well today when being part of this group?	What have I seen some-one else do well today as part of this group?
1. Think about the people around you and how they are thinking about you. Adjust your behavior to keep them thinking about you the way you want them to think about you.		
2. Establish a physical pres-ence. Use your body to show you are part of the group by maintaining a physical prox-imity, and keeping your shoulders and head turned into the group. Use body language to convey interest.		
3. Think with your eyes. Think about other people's needs with your eyes. Be aware that other people in the group are considering the focus of your eyes too.		
4. Use language to relate to other people in the group by asking questions about them, making positive comments and relating your own expe-riences to theirs.		

Define the Four Steps of Communication

1. Thinking about people and what they think and feel
   What does this mean?

2. Being aware of your physical presence as well as the physical presence of others
   What does this mean?

3. Using your eyes to think about others and see what they are thinking about
   What does this mean?

4. Using your language to relate to others
   What does this mean?

Social Spying

Page 1 of 2

I can see what other people are doing right when they do each of the Four Steps of Communication. I can also see when things don't go quite so well at times. I have thoughts about all of this.

On the following chart, I can write down when I spy a person doing one of the four steps really well. I can also write down when I see that one of the four steps could be improved! I remember that ALL people mess up these 4 steps just about every week!

Step 1: They should be thinking about the people they are talking to.	Write down two examples of kids doing this well.	Write down one example of a time when someone needed to work on this more.
Step 2: They should be keeping their bodies with the group with their head and shoulders turned into the group.	Write down two examples of kids doing this well.	Write down one example of a time when someone needed to work on this more.
Step 3: Their eyes should show that they are thinking about the other people in the group.	Write down two examples of kids doing this well.	Write down one example of a time when someone needed to work on this more.

Social Spying

Page 2 of 2

Step 4: Their language should connect to what other people are talking about.	Write down two examples of kids doing this well.	Write down one example of a time when someone needed to work on this more.

Spying on **Yourself**

Think about all the Four Steps of Communication	Write down two examples of when you were doing them well. Was it step 1, 2, 3 of 4?	Write down one example of an area you need to work on. Is it step 1, 2, 3 or 4?

Social Thinking Happens Everywhere

Social thinking and social skills are required even when we are not friends with the people or we are not talking to the people around us.

Here are some situations when you should use social thinking and social skills:

1. Hanging out with friends

2. Working in a group at school

3. Passing kids in the halls at school

4. Sitting in class listening to others talk

5. Watching TV with your family

6. Eating meals with others

7. Being at the doctor's office

8. Waiting to order food in a restaurant

Now think of five more places where you must use social thinking and social skills:

1.

2.

3.

4.

5.

Now think of 3 places where you DON'T use social thinking and social skills even though people expect you to:

1.

2.

3.

The truth is that in every place we share with others we have to be thinking and acting socially. Everything you are learning about thinking about people and adjusting your behavior can be used just about everywhere you go! You have to be a social thinker even when you are hiking on the top of a mountain or playing video games as long as you are with other people.

Using Language to Get What You Want!

We use different types of language at different times in our friendships/relationships with others. The type of language we use to talk to people sends them hidden messages.

Remember, at the heart of talking is what you are thinking about yourself or other people. People can read some of your thoughts by what you focus on in your language.

What You Want: *To learn about others*

What You Do: *Small Talk*

When you first start to get to know a person, you are likely to use "small talk." Small talk is when you ask a lot of little questions to learn about the person and find out if you have anything in common. Small talk questions can be pretty standard. (e.g. What grade are you in? What teachers do you have? What do you like to do?)

It is okay to tell people a bit about yourself with comments when you are in small talk, but the real focus needs to be on learning about the other person. You want the bulk of your language to focus on the other person!

What You Want: *To maintain a friendship/acquaintance*

What You Do: *Regular Talk*

Remember things about the person you are talking to and ask them questions or make comments about what they are interested in. It is okay to say comments about yourself, but if most of your comments are about your own thoughts what signal are you sending the other person??

Using Language to Get What You Want!

What You Want: *Someone To Really Have Good Thoughts About You*

What You Do: *You talk mostly about them.*

What You Want: *Someone to think you know a lot*

What You Do *Talk on and on about topics you know a lot about.*

(This is not recommended if you want the person to like you!)

What You Want: *People to think you are pretty self-centered*

What You Do: *When ever they are talking about themselves shift the topic so that you are only talking about yourself. Or only ask them questions that have to do with what you want to talk about.*

(This is also not recommended if you want the person to like you!)

What You Want: *Someone to think you are a good listener*

What You Do: *Support the other person by making comments that show you are listening, but don't interject your own comments about you. Definitely don't tell the person what he or she should do.*

What You Want: *To manipulate someone to do something out of the ordinary for you*

What You Do: *Start by focusing on the other person. Compliment him or her and talk about him or her. Then tell this person your problem and see if he or she volunteers to help you.*

Getting Mom and Dad's Attention

Mom and Dad are very busy; lots of things take up their time. Sometimes I need their help or just need to ask them a question. If I burst in when they are in a conversation or when they are working quietly, it makes them feel frustrated. No one likes to be interrupted!

When they are busy, I need to be patient. A patient response would be one where I quietly approach them and look towards them. Then I need to say "Excuse me." When one of them looks at me, I can then ask my question unless they tell me this is not a good time to be interrupted.

Mom and Dad are very busy. Things that take their time include:

1.

2.

3.

Sometimes I need to ask them a question or need their help when they are busy. Here are the steps I need to do before I interrupt them:

1.

2.

3.

4.

Doing this will make us all feel better!

Getting a Conversation Started

The hardest part about having a conversation can be getting started...

To get started you have to think about:

1. Who is it you are talking to?

2. What do you have in common?

3. What do you remember from the last time you spoke?

4. Has anything new or interesting happened in your life that could interest the other person(s)?

Practice: Pick a person in the group to think about: _____

Write a question you could ask that person based on the answers to the questions above:

_____

Write a comment you could tell that person about your own experiences to kick off a conversation:

_____

_____

Sometimes you are hanging with a group of people or a person that you really don't know. Think of four general areas of interest that you could talk about with people your age and write a comment or question to introduce each topic. For example, your teacher might talk to his or her friends about their kids, so he or she might ask, "How are your children?"

1.

2.

3.

4.

Using Question Prompts to Help Organize Your Thoughts

There are three steps you have to go through to change a single behavior:

When we are talking to others we can wonder about their lives or experiences and ask them questions. Our questions show that we are interested in people and also help us get more information about them.

As helpful as questions can be to find out about others, there are some questions that would be considered "inappropriate to ask." Brainstorm with your group about the difference between "appropriate questions" and "inappropriate questions" (those that might embarrass or annoy the person you are talking to).

There are many words or phrases we can use to start a question. Below is a sample of some of these. Use these words to help organize your thoughts about different "appropriate" questions you can ask other people.

WHO?

WHAT?

WHERE?

WHEN?

WHY?

HOW?

CAN YOU?

Learning About Other People

We find out about other people by asking QUESTIONS.

Questions are words that can start with:

WHO?
WHAT?
WHEN?
WHERE?
WHY?
HOW?
CAN YOU…?
REMEMBER WHEN…?

Once you ask a question, you then have to listen with your eyes and brain to the answer.

You can store the answer in your brain, so that you remember that information the next time you talk to that person.

Now it is time for you to learn about some of your friends in the group. Even if you have asked them questions in the past, each minute they are alive means they are experiencing different new things they can talk about. Can you think of four questions you can ask another person to learn more about him or her since the last time you saw each other?

If you need help, ask and we will help you write the questions!

1. _____

2. _____

3. _____

4. _____

NOW IT IS TIME TO ASK AND LEARN ABOUT ANOTHER PERSON!

Using Follow-Up Questions

Once you start asking people questions to find out about them, you will also want to learn how to use follow-up questions. Follow-up questions help you to find out more specific information. Follow-up questions show people that you want to learn more about the other person.

If we ask people any questions we happen to think of, there is a good chance that the questions will seem unrelated. Here is a sample list of questions that I could ask another person. But if the questions I ask each introduce a new topic, then it does not seem like I want to learn very much about that person.

1. What sports do you like?

2. What TV shows do you like?

3. Who is in your family?

4. What do you want to do this summer?

Now here is an example of asking one topic question and then using "follow-up questions" to learn more about that specific topic.

Topic Question: What's your favorite sport?

1. Do you like to play it or just watch it?

2. Who is your favorite team?

3. When was the last time you saw a game?

Now you practice:

1. Ask a person a question that introduces a new topic. You can use any of the questions above or you can think of your own.

2. Listen to the response. Think of follow-up questions related to that answer which you can ask to find out things that you do not know. Remember, you are NOT supposed to already know all about every person's life and ideas. Rather, you are supposed to try to find out about them by asking questions. Can you think of 3 follow-up questions?

3. Now ask one of your follow-up questions and then consider 2 more follow-up questions you can ask based on the answer to that question.

Targeting Asking Follow-Up Questions

Define "Follow-Up Questions"

Each time you ask a question that follows up on information you are receiving from someone else's topic of discussion, mark your progress by writing an X in a space between the lines of the target. Start on the outside and move in toward the center. When you get to the center you will have done a great job following up with questions about other people. The goal is to keep your attention focused on someone else and keep your words related to what he or she is talking about. That takes practice and more practice! Here's your target practice.

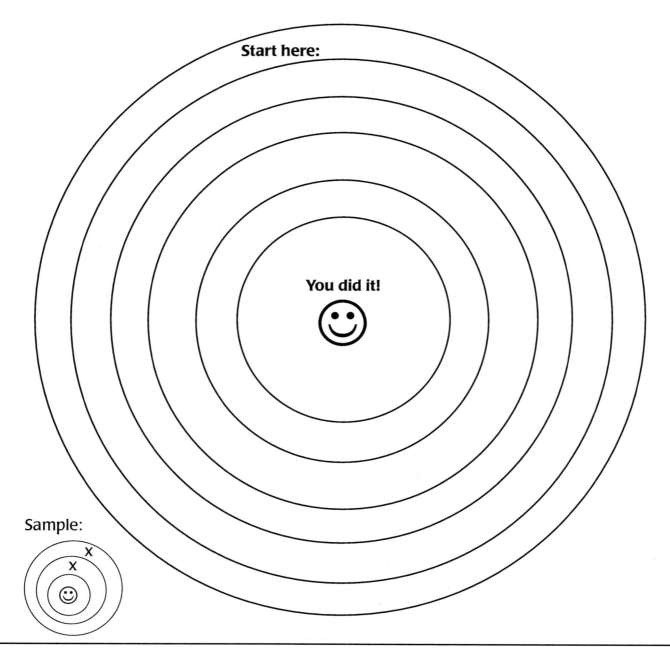

Start here:

You did it!

Sample:

Using Visualizing and Verbalizing to Inquire about Others

Think about the elements you learned to visualize and verbalize about in the Lindamood-Bell program[1] and see how they relate to questions you could ask to find out about people you are talking to.

1. Size: You can ask questions to encourage people to describe objects by size (when relevant).

2. Color: You could ask questions to explore the color of things discussed (when relevant).

3. Number: Find out the quantity.

4. Shape: Ask questions to get descriptions of how things look.

5. Where: Ask about location.

6. Movement: What were they doing?

7. Mood: How did people feel?

8. Background: What else was going on?

9. Perspective: What were people thinking?

10. When: Ask about time aspects of the event.

11. Sound: What did something sound like?

We ask these questions to get more information so we can further connect with other people's experiences. It is likely that we don't NEED this information to survive the day, but we ask questions to show interest in another person. The more we find out about a person, the more we can relate to his or her experiences. We can also use the information we learn about the person as topics to talk about during future interactions!

[1]These 11 descriptors are taken from the Lindamood Bell program *Visualizing and Verbalizing for Language Comprehension and Thinking:* www.lindamoodbell.com

131

Making Brain Videos of Things People Say

Page 1 of 2

People tell us things all the time. When they do, we have to picture what they tell us in our own "mind's eye." We can do this by making a Brain Video…

By looking at this imaginary movie in your brain, you can start to figure out what information you already know, and what information you need to make your video more complete.

When listening to another person talk, you need to make sure you are paying attention to what you know is happening in his or her life rather than make a guess about what you think should be happening. You can find out more information by asking questions.

For example, I might say "We went hiking this weekend." You then know that I went for a hike and you can picture this in your head. But…do you know WHERE we went hiking and WHO "we" are? You can find out this information by asking questions like "Where did you go hiking?" and "Who did you go with?" When I tell you that I went with my husband and my dog, you can add this to your brain's video. Now you have to figure out if you know my husband and my dog. If not, you can ask a question to make your movie even clearer. You might ask "What type of dog do you have?" Once I tell you it is a "small black wire-haired terrier that is crazy," you can add that information into your brain's video. You can then try to figure out even more information by asking "Why do you say your dog is crazy?" What you will see is that each time a piece of information is added to the video, more questions can be asked.

Brain videos help you to hold on to the information! Asking questions shows that you are interested in someone else's experience. When you show interest in others they often then want to pay more attention to you as well.

Making Brain Videos of Things People Say

Page 2 of 2

Below are some of the things that you may want to check to see if you know when other people are giving you information. If you find you want more information to make your video clearer, ask some questions!

1. WHO?
   Any questions about the people who might have been there (or who were not there!)

2. WHAT?
   Questions about the details (e.g. "What did you do in Carmel?")

3. WHERE?
   Questions about the location of events

4. WHEN?
   Questions about the time of events

5. WHY?
   Questions about why things happened the way they did

6. HOW?
   Questions about how something was done

7. WAS IT FUN?
   Questions about the quality of the experience

There are plenty more questions that can be asked...
These are just a few to get you started.

Comments…little things to tell

Comments are thoughts we add to a discussion to show people we are listening, have thoughts, and even have some new ideas to contribute to the discussion.

Comments can be small thoughts we add to other people's statements. They allow people to get a better idea about what we are thinking.

But if our comments get tooooooooooo long, then it is hard for people to keep listening because their ears get tired! They also might think that the speaker is more interested in talking than in learning about other people.

Comments are only interesting to other people if we also take time to listen to what they want to tell us! Once you are done with your comment, listen to the other people's ideas too…

Now it is time to practice:

⊙ Talk to the group about one place you really like to visit or one thing you really like to do. Keep your comments short (15-30 seconds maximum). The teacher can use a timer to cut off the speaker with a two-second warning.

⊙ Talk to the group about one place you really like to visit or one thing you really like to do and this time talk for a much longer time (about 1 minute).

⊙ As a group, discuss if the group was better able to stay interested in the longer or the shorter comments.

⊙ Practice longer and shorter timed comments about a variety of topic such as:

  • Favorite foods

  • Places you hate to go with your family

  • Favorite things about school

  • Things you like to do during the summer

Compliments Make People Feel Good

COMPLIMENTS are words that are said to tell people you like something about them.

You can compliment people for a bunch of different reasons. For example you can:

Compliment them on what they wear... "I like your baseball hat."
Compliment them on what they say... "That is a good idea!"
Compliment them on what they do... "Your picture looks cool!"

Compliments show that you are thinking about someone else. People like it when others notice good things about them. Saying compliments to people helps them to notice how cool you are!!

Today we are working on cooperating together. When we play together, compliments make the play friendlier for everyone. Compliments also may make people more willing to be helpful to you.

Today let's practice giving compliments!

Write down one compliment about the person sitting on your right side...

_____

Here are some important rules about using compliments:

1. Do not interrupt what people are saying to give them a compliment.
2. Don't give someone too many compliments. Too many compliments can make people wonder why you are being so nice.

There are other ways to make people feel good besides giving compliments. These include showing interest in what other people are saying and asking questions about them.

Add Your Thought to Their Thought

"Social Communication" is when you are talking with people you know just for the fun of being with other people.

The purpose of social communication is to give the other people some information about you that helps them to know more about you. But, the information you give them is supposed to be given…

QUICKLY and JUST A LITTLE BIT AT A TIME (but NOT TOO LITTLE)

It is supposed to be quick because communication looks like it is breaking down if it takes longer than 1-2 seconds for you to get started adding your own thoughts.

It is supposed to be *"JUST A LITTLE BIT AT A TIME"* because people can learn only so much at once. And if you tell them everything, it doesn't give them anything to talk to you or question you about.

When people ask you questions, what you want to avoid is telling them NOTHING! If someone says, "What did you do last night?" and you say "NOTHING," that doesn't give the other person anything to think about!!!

One more really important thing! When the reason people are talking to each other is for social communication, what they talk about is NOT VERY IMPORTANT. The topics are something that anybody should be able to add-a-thought to. The topics rarely are about teaching really smart facts about the world. Instead social communication teaches us how to understand and relate to different people. You do not have to be very smart about a topic in order to be able to add your own thought to the topic during social communication. For example, what thought could you add if people are talking about... frogs, new cars, dogs, hair brushes, peacocks, airplanes, teddy bears, staplers, toilet paper, backpacks, television programs, hair spray, bathing suits, toasters, cups, socks, mold on toes, etc…?

Practice adding your thoughts to weird topics. You will find out you have so much to say!

Add-a-Thought to Connect to People's Words

People often tell us a little bit about what they are thinking. Then we need to show that we are listening to them and want to learn more about them. To do this we ask questions or make comments about what they tell us. But we don't have to focus on the other people the whole time; we can add our own thoughts and experiences to what they are talking about as long as we still show that we are interested in them. This is what a "Thinking of You" person would do.

Sometimes we just seem to keep talking about ourselves and we don't act like we really care what the other people are saying. People who act like "Just MEs" always seem to talk about themselves.

1. Think of how to respond to each of the comments below to show you are thinking about the other person.

2. Then, create a response that a "JUST ME" person would say.

For example: If I said, "I didn't feel well last night!" a "THINKING OF YOU" person might ask, "What was wrong?" or "Do you feel well now?" Or he or she might just say, "That's a bummer." "A "JUST ME" person might say, "I felt fine last night." or "I was sick during vacation."

a. My dog was really bad over the holidays.
b. I had a bad weekend.
c. I really want a new game boy game.
d. I am playing in a chess tournament.
e. I was sick this weekend.
f. I had fun last night.
g. I had a hard test.
h. My lunch was terrible.
i. My friend was mean.
j. I had fun at recess.
k. My teacher looked so weird today.
l. I wish it was vacation!
m. My sister broke her arm.
n. I don't like school.
o. I had so much fun in PE.
p. I am on level 6 of a computer game.
q. Our class is going on a field trip.
r. This kid got hurt on the playground today.
s. My birthday is next week.
t. My birthday was yesterday.

Add-a-Thought to Connect to People's Words

Now list five things you noticed or experienced, good or bad, in the last few days that you can comment on and people can respond to, about you.

Examples: "My dog was terrible on Christmas Day." or "I did not have a great weekend." or "I saw a good movie."

1._____

2._____

3._____

4._____

5._____

Another person is to take the information you wrote above and generate at least 3 different ways he or she could ask a question or make a comment about each comment that you wrote. Remember, it is okay to share some of your own experiences especially if you also show people that you understand how they are feeling.

For example, if a person did say "My dog was terrible on Christmas Day." you could say:

1. "That's too bad; did he destroy some of the gifts?"
2. "What did your dog do?"
3. "That's a bummer; my dog is too old to do anything bad anymore."

A "Just ME" might say, "I had a great Christmas."

Add-a-Thought When Playing

When people are playing together they use words to glue their play together. These words show that they are thinking about the game and the people playing the game.

Saying good thoughts you are having about other people when you play with them shows them that you are thinking good things about them!

All people like some compliments!
But...**BEWARE! Too many compliments make people feel weird.**

Adding a comment about what you are playing helps other people learn more about what you like and what you are thinking. Comments that connect in some way to the play help us to learn about each other.

But...**BEWARE! Comments that talk about things that have nothing to do with the play make it seem like you are not interested in what you are playing.**

(These are called whopping topic changes!)

We are now going to practice playing and talking.

We are going to focus on what we are saying when we play together!

Supporting And Add-A-Thought Comments And Questions

When conversing, our job is to show interest in what others are talking about while also trying to keep the conversation interesting for us as well! That can be hard. Here are two ways in which we participate in a conversation.

1. Using Supporting Questions and Comments:

A. Supporting comments are comments that support what someone else is already saying. You do not change the topic to what you are interested in when you use this type of comment. For example, if I tell you I went to a great Asian restaurant this weekend, you could make a supporting comment like, "That sounds really good." Now think of a different supporting comment to say: _____

_____

B. Supporting questions are questions that support what someone else is saying. You do not take over the topic and change it to what you want to talk about when you ask this type of question. For example, if I tell you my kids went to see the "Ocean's 11" movie this weekend, you could ask a supporting question like, "Did they like it?" Now try asking another supporting question: _____

_____

2. Add-a-Thought Comments and Questions:

A. Add-a-thought comments are comments that connect to what someone else is saying. At the same time these comments introduce a thought about what you like to talk about. For example, if I tell you my kids went to the movie "Ocean's 11" this weekend, you could add your own thoughts in a comment like, "I went to my brother's football game this weekend." Now think of another add-a-thought comment you could say:

_____

_____

B. Add-a-thought (or bridging) questions are questions that connect to what someone else is saying, but they allow you to ask about something that you are interested in that is related to that topic. For example, if I tell you I went to a great Asian restaurant this weekend, you could ask a bridging question like "Have you ever been to the Asian Garden restaurant?" Now think of a bridging question you could ask:

_____

_____

What do supporting comments and questions do in a conversation? What do add-a thought comments and bridging questions do in a conversation? How do you know which to use?

Choosing Your Words Carefully!

Talking is kind of like fishing; your words serve as the "bait" that helps to keep people "reeled in" to the conversation or discussion. When we introduce a new topic to talk about, we can say we "put out the bait." Often we "put out the bait" and then add a related comment or question to elaborate on our message.

Subtle differences in how we word these follow-up comments and questions can make other people want to join our topic... or not. So we need to choose our words carefully, just like you have to choose your bait carefully to lure the fish!

Here are some examples of "putting out the bait" and following it up with some comments and questions which could work well to keep the conversation going. There are also examples of comments and questions which usually don't make people want to talk about our topic. Discuss how each of these techniques impacts the listeners.

Bait and Brag: *(this is NOT a good skill)*

This is where you introduce a topic and then tell people how wonderful you are! This does not usually make people feel good about you since bragging makes you sound like you think you are superior to your listeners.

• I went shopping this weekend at Stanford Mall. I got so many new clothes; they were all from really nice stores.

• I exercised this weekend everyday for at least an hour. I hiked, played basketball, and went snowboarding. I'm really good at all those sports.

• I had a test so I studied a whole bunch. I think I got an "A." How do you think you did?•

• I stayed home and read some books. I read about one book every two days. I think books are much more interesting than people.

Bait and Comment:

This is where you introduce a topic and then you comment about it, but not in a way that makes you look fabulous.

• I went shopping this weekend at Stanford Mall.

• I exercised outdoors a lot this weekend. I was so glad it didn't rain during the day.

• I studied a bunch for a test. I hate tests.

• I read some books while over vacation. I read a really interesting science fiction book.

Choosing Your Words Carefully!

Bait and Support:

This is where you introduce the topic but then you want to find out what other people think.

- I went shopping this weekend at the Stanford Mall. Do you like to go there?

- I exercised outdoors a lot this weekend. What did you do?

- Did you worry much about the test today in math? You seem really good in that class.

- I read some books over vacation. What did you do?

Monitor the comments made by people in the group and determine which type of question or comment they use after they "put out the bait" (introduce a new topic).

Write down or discuss some examples of what you heard yourself or other people use:

Bait and brag:

Bait and comment:

Bait and support.

How do you feel about each of these types of comments? Which will you practice using?

Which way are we speaking, Tangent or Topic?

Going off on a Tangent – the Definition:

• At least one of the speakers goes off on a topic that is very loosely related to what we were talking about.

• At times it is hard for the listener to follow how the conversation got from one topic to the next.

• At times the listener can follow the tangent but doesn't understand how it really relates to the general topic under discussion.

• At times the listener understands how it relates but gets frustrated because the speaker doesn't seem to be interested in what the other person had to say.

Staying on Topic – the Definition:

• The listener can follow what the speaker is talking about.

• The listener feels like the speaker is interested in him or her.

• The speaker makes comments which show that he or she understands what the listener has experienced or how he or she feels.

Ways of Talking That People DO NOT Appreciate

Whopping Topic Change = "WTC"

A whopping topic change is when a person makes a comment that is not related to what people are talking about and people cannot figure out how that person's brain got to that thought.

An example of a WTC would be if a group was talking about their favorite restaurants and a person started to describe a video game that he or she likes to play. In this case people could not figure out the connection, unless someone was talking about video games at a restaurant.

Tangent Talk = "TT"

Often in conversations people go off on tangents. A tangent is when people can see how your comment relates to the topic but it was not the main idea of the topic. Tangent talk can be accepted as not being a problem when people are just hanging out and adding their thoughts just for the fun of it and no one is talking about anything too serious.

Tangent talk will be less tolerated when the people who are talking have a clear purpose for their conversation and they also have some time limitations for the discussion. When a teacher is leading a discussion in class she really wants everyone to keep their comments close to the topic so that the students can keep their brains focused and learn the main idea she or he is trying to teach.

There are also times in a conversation when a person is really trying to explain something that he or she is thinking or feeling. If someone else keeps making tangential comments, then it feels to the main speaker that the other person is not interested in what he or she has to say.

Here is an example of tangent talk that **doesn't** work. One person is talking about how worried she is about letting her parents see her report card and the other person just talks about the fact that the paper that the report cards are printed on should come from recycled sources.

Different Types of Communication for Different Purposes

Page 1 of 4

First you have to figure out why you are talking to the person before you can figure out how best to communicate with him or her.

• Is it just to socialize?

• Is it because you want something from him or her (e.g. lunch money, to copy homework, to compare answers?)

• Is it so he or she can help you solve a problem or learn some new information?

• Are you trying to make a good impression for a club, committee or job interview?

Here are some thoughts on different ways to communicate depending on what you want from the situation. Remember you always need to consider how the other person might be interpreting what you are saying or doing.

If you are meeting someone for the first or second or third time, you really want to make sure that you focus your attention on that person:

• Find out about the person.

• Ask the person questions about what he or she enjoys.

• Say things about yourself that relate to what the person is interested in so that he or she can connect with you.

• When the person asks you questions about yourself, only give a little bit of information at first. If the person is interested in finding out more about you, then he or she will ask you more questions.

• If you notice that you are talking a lot and the person is not asking any questions or maintaining really active listening, then you may be talking too much!

• If the person tells you about how he or she is feeling, make note of it and comment on it in a way that supports him or her! If the person just failed a test, a good thing to do is to say that it is a bummer and that you know how bad that feels. If instead you say, "I just got an A." you are not helping that person to like you!

Section 6: Developing Effective Communication   145   © Michelle Garcia Winner 2005 • www.socialthinking.com

Different Types of Communication for Different Purposes

If you have known the person a while and he or she is considered to be one of your better friends:

- You can more openly express your personal opinion.

- You can more easily talk about things of interest to you.

- Use a lot of add-a-thoughts to connect your thoughts to that person's thoughts! Always avoid whopping topic change!

- You can NEVER stop monitoring how that person is interpreting what you say and do! Once a friendship starts, it has to be heavily maintained! You still have to be very careful about how much you talk about yourself.

- Pay close attention to the person's emotions. If the person tells you how he or she is feeling, listen up! Try to get a feeling for what he or she must be feeling. Good friends give a strong sense of emotional relatedness!

If you want something from one of your friends/peers:

- Spend almost all your talking time focused on the other person. Show strong interest in what he or she is talking about.

- Keep asking questions about what he or she likes.

- Don't be too quick to talk with this person about what you want from him or her. If you do, the person will think you are "using" him or her. Be subtle in your request; tell the person indirectly about your problem. For example, if you forgot to do your homework say, "Hey, did we have homework in math last night?"... "Oh man, I totally forgot about it! My mom is going to kill me!" At this point the person may volunteer to let you see his or her homework. If that doesn't happen, you can ask "Can you help me out with this?" If the answer is "NO," then you need to leave it alone. Don't respond with anger. (It is your problem, not his or hers!) Instead, say something like, "That's cool, I understand." If you put a lot of pressure on the person, he or she will really start to dislike you. If you are asking to borrow money and the person lets you, MAKE SURE YOU PAY THE MONEY BACK!

- Make sure you treat the person well after he or she does a favor for you!

Different Types of Communication for Different Purposes

If you are talking to a person who is going to help you solve a problem or teach you something:

- Initially say "hi" and ask how that person is doing. If the person seems really rushed, let him or her know that you want to talk but you realize this might not the best time. If the person agrees that it is not a good time, ask when a good time would be. Show up promptly at the agreed upon time.

- Stay focused on what you need help with. This is not a discussion which is intended to be social, so avoid discussing your own personal life.

- Pay attention to what the person is telling you! Almost all people are happy to help, but if people have to help you with the same problem over and over again, they don't feel like they are helping anymore…and then they are not so happy.

- Let the person know if you need time to write down what he or she is telling you. It is even okay to ask the person to write out the information for you.

- Keep your eyes and language focused on the discussion!

- Repeat what the person has told you to make sure that you have interpreted it correctly.

- It is a really good idea to ask a question if something doesn't make sense to you. It is best to ask the question right when you realize you are confused.

- If the person is talking too fast, it is okay to ask him or her to slow down. Let the person know that it is confusing or hard for you and it is not his or her fault for talking too fast. (All people are very sensitive and don't like to be blamed by others for doing things wrong!)

- Follow through on the information you are given to help solve your problem. If you don't try to go solve your problem or do your work after the person has taken time to work with you, he or she may not be willing to help you in the future!

- Remember… people are internally wired to want to help other people. It makes them feel good!

Different Types of Communication for Different Purposes

If you are trying to make a good impression because you are joining a club, interviewing for a job, etc:

- Remember that your physical presence communicates more about yourself than your words! Focus on how you look (your clothes) as well as your body language and facial expression.

- Show the other people that you are interested in them by looking at them and having a pleasant look on your face.

- Pay close attention to what other people are saying. They may ask you questions and you want to give answers that relate exactly to what they are talking about. (Do not give tangential responses!)

- If you did not understand what someone said, you can ask the person to repeat the question.

- Try to avoid literally interpreting all the questions. Think about what the person really means by his or her question. For example, if someone asks you, "What are your weaknesses?" don't say that you are not very good at swimming if you are interviewing for a job at "Target." The person would only want to know about what would be difficult for you when working in that setting. When you answer, don't just tell negative things about yourself. Follow them with something positive. For example, if you say, "Getting organized is difficult for me." back it up with "But I keep learning how to do this better."

- Do not share your own strong personal opinions unless you have already been accepted into the group. For example, if someone asks you how you feel about teamwork, say "It is really important when working with others to work as a team." Don't say, "It is a waste of time." Anytime you are trying to become part of a group (which includes trying to get a job) you have to realize that other people think teamwork and group discussion are important.

Small Talk

Making small talk means asking questions and giving short responses about topics that most people are comfortable discussing. Small talk never involves very serious topics or heavy discussions. Small talk topics that are not too serious might include the weather, a movie you saw, how fun your vacation was, or how your school day went.

Why do we bother with small talk?

1. It helps people get to know each other.

2. It makes people feel at ease or comfortable.

3. By providing an introduction to an array of topics, small talk can help start a conversation.

Some Small Talk Topics

Weather, Health, Travel, Work or School, Entertainment, Free Time, Activities, Food, Family, Vacations, Holiday Plans, Pets, etc…

Can you think of two more?

To Get To Know Someone...
Start with Small Talk

Small talk consists of those little questions you ask to find out general information about a person. Often the topic during small talk changes rapidly since the answers given are pretty short. Why do you think people do small talk?

Steps Toward Small Talk:

Step 1: Before you start talking, look at the person.

- Is he or she wearing anything that indicates a hobby or interest? (e.g. a t-shirt with a topic on it, a pin, or special jewelry)

- What is the person's age and gender? A person's gender and age give you clues as to what he or she might be interested in, such as TV shows that that person might watch.

Step 2: Given what you see, what might this person might be interested in talking about?

1. _____

_____

2. _____

_____

3. _____

_____

Step 3: Think of questions you would ask to start to engage this person in small talk?

1. _____

_____

2. _____

_____

3. _____

_____

To Get To Know Someone…
Start with Small Talk

Page 2 of 2

Moving on to a Conversation:

A conversation is a deeper discussion during which you stay with one topic for a while, or it can involve each person taking turns talking about a strand of related topics.

• The conversation usually starts with one person asking the other person a question or by one person making a comment about something he or she experienced.

• Each person can then add a comment or ask the other a question to keep the conversation going.

• People can keep conversations moving by adding thoughts to topics being discussed. It is actually possible to carry on conversations just by having each person make related comments.

• During conversations all people are both speakers and listeners; it is important for each person to do both! If you only speak, people don't think you care about them. If you only listen, people wonder if you are really interested.

Discuss or write down your thoughts about the following questions:

Why are conversations important to friendships?

_____

What is "turn-taking?"

_____

Why is it important to be both speaker and listener?

_____

How can comments about your own life add to a conversation?

_____

Why is it important to think about the person you are talking to before you start talking to him or her?_____

_____

Section 6: Developing Effective Communication   151   © Michelle Garcia Winner 2005 • www.socialthinking.com

Thinking About Other People
Before You Talk to Them

First your brain has to think about WHO you are talking to.
Then it has to think about what THEY would like to talk about.

List your friends' names:	1. Name:	2. Name:	3. Name:	How would a friend answer these questions about you?
What do you remember about this person?				
What do you think this person would like to talk about?				
What is a question you could ask him or her?				

Conversation Starters

We organize our thoughts even in conversations. We start all conversations by thinking about who we are talking to. We also need to consider what they might want to talk about.

Let's consider the many different ways you can start to organize a conversation. What are questions you can ask or comments you can say about the following topics?

Seasonal topics	Where the person spends much of his/her day (school, job, home)	Hobbies	Interests or movies	Family or shared friends	Prior shared experiences	Things you are planning to do or hope to do with this person

Thinking About What to Tell Others So They Will Still Want to Listen

People are easily overwhelmed with information. There are a few key things to consider when talking to others:

1. Communication should start quickly (within 1-2 seconds) and information should be to the point, especially in a more formal group. (e.g. classroom, meeting)

2. While you are talking, you have to consider what people already know and don't know.

3. Your message should contain only the relevant information people need or want to know.

What are all the things I could tell you about the following topics?	What are just the main points I should tell you so I don't tell you too much!
Hobbies:	
Homework:	
Foods I like:	
Answering a teacher's question in science class:	
(Pick your own topic)	
(Pick your own topic)	

Responding to What People Say

People ask us questions or make comments that imply that we should respond.

Responding to a question:

It is obvious that when someone asks us a direct question we should respond. It is not as obvious who should respond when someone asks a question to everyone in the group. If the person is looking at you, that is a strong clue that he or she is asking you the question. If the speaker is looking at someone else, he or she IS NOT asking you the question. If the speaker is looking a little bit at everyone, then anyone can answer.

Responding to comments:

An example of a comment that implies one should respond might be when someone who is talking about his or her dog gets to the end of the story, stops talking, and looks at you. You should then respond by connecting your thought to that person's thought by saying something like, "I wish I had a dog like that."

Rules of Responding:

Once you know you are to respond, there are some general rules to follow. (Be aware, though, that there will be times when these rules won't apply. You always have to stay very alert to see when that happens.)

1. Speed is critical. You have about 1-2 seconds to respond after someone says something to you in order for communication to stay healthy and active.

   When someone asks you what your FAVORITE thing to do is, he or she doesn't actually mean your ALL TIME FAVORITE. What the person means for you to do is quickly tell something you kind of like. It does not have to be your all time favorite thing, because to consider what your favorite thing of all time is may take way too much time!

   Another example of this might be when someone asks you what your favorite movie is. The person doesn't really mean your actual favorite. He or she is just asking the name of one movie that you liked or for you to tell what general type of movies you like. To think about your actual favorite movie takes so much thinking time that it slows communication down too much.

2. Verbal communication lacks precision and is often a bit sloppy. Since speed is such a factor, you get to slack off on speaking in perfect grammar.

3. In answering a question, give some specific information so that your answer gives the other person something to think about. This helps him or her to think of new things to say to you. For example, someone asks what you did this weekend. If you tell the person one or two things you did (even if they were not really exciting events) you give him or her something to connect to and think about. However, if you respond by saying "Nothing," you give the person nothing to think about, and this kills the conversation.

Responding to What People Say

Page 2 of 2

Rules of Responding (continued):

4. While you don't want to respond to a question by saying "nothing," you also want to be sure you don't do the opposite and give a response that is too long. Responses should generally be no longer than 30 seconds. A research study of teenage boys talking together showed that there were usually five different comments made within one minute of conversation.

5. If you give a response and the other person asks another question about your topic, he or she is showing some interest in what you have to say. You can then give him or her a bit more information. If you give too little information in your response, the other person has to keep asking questions in order to get enough information to understand what you are talking about. This puts a lot of work on your communication partner and it can appear that you don't want to talk to him or her. For example, someone might ask you, "Do you have a pet?" and you say, "Yeah, a dog." If the person then asks for more information like, "What kind of dog?" or "How old is it?" then you should give the person a bit more information to paint a picture about your dog in his or her brain so that he or she has more to think about.

6. Only tell people what they don't already know. This means you need to be very aware of what the person you are talking to might be thinking or have some knowledge about. If you don't know how much he or she knows about a topic, ask. For example, you might say "I really like to study black holes. Do you know much about them?" If the person says "Yeah, I read a book on it." then you would not tell that person what a black hole is. Instead you would discuss your fascination with the topic because that would be information he or she would not already know.

7. Only give more information on a topic if the other person seems interested in the topic. Imagine you brought up the topic of black holes as in the example above. If the person said, "Stuff like that never really interests me." this means that he or she really doesn't want you to talk about that topic. This would be a good time to switch the topic to one that you know the other person is interested in.

Summary of Rules for Responding:

1. Respond quickly (1-2 seconds).

2. Don't worry about your grammar.

3. Don't say "nothing" and don't give too much information.

4. Keep responses to 30 seconds or less.

5. Don't make your conversational partner work too hard to get information from you.

6. Only give information the listener doesn't already know.

7. If the listener isn't interested in the topic, change the topic.

One More Tip:

You DO NOT want to talk about controversial topics when you are just meeting someone for the first time. We usually stay with neutral topics when we first meet people. (Avoid politics, religion, violence, disgusting humor, etc.)

Steps for Acknowledging and Getting to Know Others

…whether you want to be their friend or just not have them dislike you!

1. Keep your head up and observe people. Realize that you have a choice as to who you may want to talk to in a group.

2. Determine the following:

      a. Do you know anyone here?

      b. Who looks like someone that you might like to get to know?

3. If you want to get to know a person, or if you see someone you know, look in his or her direction from time to time.

4. Say "Hi" to any and everyone who looks in your direction or looks at you while passing you.

5. Approach a person you want to talk to (this is especially true if people are just "hanging out") or sit near a person in the classroom who you may enjoy.

6. Make sure you acknowledge the person by saying "Hi," or at least sustaining eye contact with him or her while you give a small smile and head nod.

7. There are really predictable questions you can ask people when you first meet them, especially when the meeting happens in an environment that you share (e.g. school, work, roommate).

      a. How's the class going?

      b. Did you have a good weekend?

      c. What are you doing this weekend?

      d. Etc…

8. Remember what they tell you! The next time you see them, inquire about how they are based on what you remember?

Here's what NOT TO DO…

Do not think that since you have no defined relationship with a person you do not have to say hi or ask basic questions about his or her life! This is especially true with a roommate or a person you see a lot at school or on the job.

Here's the most IMPORTANT thing to remember…

ALL COMMUNICATION HAS A PURPOSE, even if the purpose is just to show another person that you are aware of him or her.

Think Of Things You Did This Weekend

1. Think of one thing that you got to do at home that you liked:

_____

2. Think of one place that you went this weekend:

_____

3. Think of one thing you wish you could have done this weekend:

_____

Now… we are each going to imagine and act out activities that someone else in the group did or wanted to do last weekend.

1. Think about one of the things someone else did or wanted to do and imagine having done it yourself.

2. While you are imagining doing the activity you have to "wonder" what it was like. Ask the person who generated the idea questions so that you can get a better sense of what they were thinking about the activity.

3. Now act it out. The person who had the experience gets to be the director of the scene.

4. After acting it out, what comments do you or other members of the group have?

Conversations with friends are a lot like imagining and acting things out, but without all the movement. You have to picture in your head what the other person is thinking and talking about and then you have to ask questions or make comments related to that person's experience!

Using People The Way They Are Intended To Be Used!

Asking For Help And Clarification

Page 1 of 2

When students go to school to learn new things, it is expected that they don't understand all the information or how to do all assignments. Teachers assume students will fill in the gaps in their knowledge by asking for help or clarification because…

• All students have times when they don't know exactly what the teacher expects or even what the teacher is trying to teach

• All students are human and they don't always pay attention the whole time

• All teachers are human and at times they do not make the assignment clear to all students

Asking for Clarification:

When a student has the general idea of what is being taught but is confused about one or two particular aspects, this is the time to ask for clarification. Students usually ask for clarification when they are part of the whole class. They raise a hand and look at the teacher to get the teacher's attention. The teacher generally answers the question right when it is asked. Usually some others in the class are happy that the question was asked since they were confused too. Sometimes asking for clarification means you just repeat what the teacher said to make sure you heard it correctly.

Task: Let's practice asking for clarification.

Think of some times in class when you have thought that the teacher did not clearly explain the assignment. What would you ask to request clarification in these situations?

Using People The Way They Are Intended To Be Used!

Asking For Help And Clarification

Page 2 of 2

Asking for Help:

When a student thinks that he has really missed out on an important piece of information because he is feeling confused or doesn't know how to get started with an assignment, he or she usually needs help. Asking for help often requires a bit more personal attention than asking for clarification. There are some good times to ask for help and some not-so-good times.

Good times to ask for help would be...

• When the teacher is having the class work on an assignment during class time and the teacher is not directly teaching the class

• When you have arranged with the teacher to meet him or her during some part of the day when he or she is not teaching a class

• When the teacher has "office hours" - this is a time when anyone can drop in and ask the teacher a question

• When you are taking a test and you do not understand what a question means

Times when it is not good to ask for a careful, individualized explanation include...

• When the teacher is giving a classroom lecture, at which point she or he is sharing her or his attention with the whole class and cannot not deal with individual concerns

• When the class is doing group work but someone in the class is causing a problem and the teacher has to deal with that child at that moment You can ask for help by both raising your hand and looking at the teacher to try to get his or her attention. You can also approach the teacher's table and stand near her or him until the teacher has time to give you some attention. When approaching the teacher, it is a good idea to look toward the teacher much of the time you are waiting.

You are also supposed to ask for help and clarification at home from your parents, a friend who is in the class, or from a sibling who has taken the class. When you do this you do not raise your hand, but you approach the person and ask if he or she has a moment to help you. If that person does have time, you try to explain what it is the teacher said and what you are confused about. Your parent, friend or sibling will need more information than the teacher since they don't exactly know what you are learning in class at that time.

TASK: Let's practice asking for help at school and at home.

Think of some times at school or at home when you were really not sure what you were supposed to do, how you were supposed to do it, or what someone meant by what he or she said. How would you go about getting someone's attention in order to ask for help? Being careful not to blame the person you are talking to, what words could you say to explain that you do not understand what you are supposed to do?

Seeking Information from Others

We ask for "help" when we are stuck or feeling overwhelmed. People are usually very happy to provide help since in general people like to feel useful to others.

We ask for "clarification" when we understand the general idea but a few details may be confusing us. People are very happy to provide clarification since all people like to feel like they are helping others succeed.

Successful people ask for help and clarification. Successful people know that no one becomes successful completely on his or her own. Successful people may not be super smart in the topic they are working on, but they are smart because they ask people questions to help them learn more about the topic or activity.

Students who get good grades often ask for help and clarification when they first start to feel uncomfortable. Often they don't completely understand what they are doing. Or they think, "What I think I need to do next really doesn't make sense to me." Then they know they should ask a question.

There is no such thing as a "dumb question."

Think of some examples of situations when you would need to ask for help and then think of situations when you would need to ask for clarification. Discuss the differences in these situations:

Asking for HELP	Asking for CLARIFICATION

Getting More Information
When You Aren't Sure What To Do!

People tell you what to do a lot!

What are some things teachers tell you to do?

To figure out if you really know how to do what teachers are telling you to do, you have to be able to answer the following questions:

1. What is the assignment or activity? (Where do I keep track of this?)

2. When is it due?

3. What do I need to get it done? Do I need extra books or extra supplies like poster paper?

4. How long is it supposed to be?

5. Am I supposed to do it by myself or work with a partner?

Start by asking yourself these questions in your head. If you are not sure about the answers to the questions, or you know the answers but you are just not sure how to do the next step, then ask a question. For example, people may know they are supposed to work with a partner, but they don't know how to find a partner. In this case, ask your teacher for help in finding a partner.

To help you practice, I am going to give you an assignment to do in our group today. If you are not sure about any part of it, you need to ask me questions to get help.

Things to remember when asking for help:

1. Think about the person you want to talk with.

2. Walk up to that person (but don't get closer or farther than an arm's distance from him or her).

3. Think with your eyes. Is the person you need to talk to busy? If so, stand by him or her and wait. Look at that person on occasion, but do not stare.

4. When the person is looking at you and not talking to anyone else, it probably means he or she is ready to talk with you.

5. Ask your question, and then think about that person with your eyes again. Think to yourself, "Did he or she understand my question?"

6. Even people you ask for help sometimes have trouble listening. If you feel that he or she did not understand your question, say "I am not sure if you understand what I am asking." Then try asking it in a slightly different way.

7. Listen for the person's response and then go do what he or she told you!

Making Phone Calls: the Basics

Page 1 of 3

There are different types of phone calls:

1. Social calls

2. Calls to someone you know to request information

3. Calls to businesses for information

The content of what you say and the message you are sending the person on the other end of the line are different for each type of phone call. Information about this is reviewed in the chart below:

Type of phone call	General content of the call	The message you give the other person	The reasons people are concerned about making these calls
Social calls	You call someone who you consider to be a friend or a friendly acquaintance to just "check in" and find out how he or she is doing. These calls are very much like conversations; you can talk about anything.	You are interested in being his or her friend. (This is a compliment to almost all people; we feel good when people take the time to show us they are thinking about us.)	• You don't know if you are intruding on a person when you can not see what he or she is doing. • You can't see how that person is reacting to you.
Calls to someone you know to ask for some information	You call a person you are familiar with, if only as an acquaintance. You start out by being friendly and exchanging some short social comments or questions like "How are you?" Then you ask the person the question you have about your homework/the meeting time/etc. You don't start by just immediately asking for the information you want because if you do, it does not seem like you are interested in the person.	You are aware of this person and respect his or her knowledge. You realize that people generally like being able to help others.	• You are not sure the person has the information. • You may be nervous calling someone that may not remember who you are. (In this case, explain how the person knows you before you proceed.) • You cannot read the person's body language.
Calls to a business for information	You call the phone number of the business and talk to whoever answers the phone to try to find out the answer to your question. You may be told to "hold" while you are transferred to someone else. You then may have to repeat your question all over again. When you first call you may not get a person at all; you may just get a recorded message. Then you will need to listen to the options listed and choose the one which will most likely be able to answer your question.	You need information and would like it as efficiently as possible. (There is almost no social chit-chat in these calls.)	• You have no idea who you are talking to. • You may have difficulty getting the listener to understand your question, so you may have to repeat yourself or slightly modify the question to help the person. • You may have difficulty understanding the recorded message options.

Making Phone Calls: the Basics

Initiating a Social or Social-Information Call

1. Initial greeting and question: After dialing the phone number, you listen to someone pick up the phone. This person is the first to speak by saying "hi." You then ask the listener, "May I please talk to _____?" This helps to clarify who you would like to speak to. If the person who answers the phone is the person you want to speak to, it is perfectly fine to still ask the question just to make sure that you are talking to the correct person.

2. Identifying yourself: Once it is clear that you have the person on the phone that you called to speak to, you then identify yourself by saying, "Hi, this is _____." Sometimes the person who answers the phone may ask for your identification by asking, "May I ask who is calling?" It is fine to give the person your name at that point.

3. Asking a question after the initial greeting: Often the caller then asks how the other person is doing. So at this point you might say something like, "How is your day going?" or "Do you have a lot of home-work?"

4. When both people have acknowledged each other on the phone, then the caller should give some indication for why he or she is calling.

   a. For a social call you can say something like, "I was just calling to see what you are up to?" This lets the person know that you are just calling to chat. From that point on the call progresses much the same way as when you are with the person face to face. Be aware of subtle cues that let you know when the person needs to get off the phone. These cues may sound something like, "I have a lot of homework to do tonight so I don't have much time to talk." or "My mom is really bugging me to get off the phone." or "I just have a minute to talk." People usually avoid being blunt about their need to get off the phone since blunt comments are interpreted as rude. A blunt comment might be, "I can't talk right now. Bye."

   b. For social-information calls you can say something like, "I was wondering if you know what our math homework is for tonight?" or "What book did our English teacher say we had to read?" The trick to asking for this information is to NOT ask for it immediately or bluntly. If you do, it appears that you are not interested in the person at all and you just want the information. Once you do get the information you want, it is okay to clarify the information by repeating it back to the person you called. At this point, the caller can thank the person and then hang up. But it is also an option to then move toward a more social phone call. One way to do this would be to say, "Thanks for the information. What are you doing tonight?" Then you transition into more of a conversation.

5. Ending a call: You MUST exit a social call by saying "Goodbye." or "See you later." or "Thanks again for the information. Bye." Even if you are in a hurry or happen to be frustrated, you should not just hang up. That is called "being hung up on" and it is seen as a sign of immense anger on the part of the person who hangs up without saying goodbye.

Making Phone Calls: the Basics

Page 3 of 3

Initiating a Business Call

Since you are calling someone at a business, you can skip all the social salutations. In this type of call you listen for a person to pick up the phone and say "Hello" and then you say "Hi" and immediately state your question (e.g. "Hi, what time does your store close?" or "Hi, I have some questions about a computer I bought there.") It is very likely that the person will put you on hold while you are transferred to someone else who the person thinks can better answer the question. Be patient and be very willing to repeat your question to multiple people. But if you get frustrated, just hang up when you are on hold. The people you are calling do not know you. They will not recognize you if they see you, so it is okay to just hang up if you feel overwhelmed. You can call back and try to get the information you need once you feel calm again.

Talking on the phone is a really important part of developing independence and friend-ships. Most people are nervous about making calls at one time or another. It is impor-tant to practice making phone calls to help you feel more confident in this more distant form of communication.

Work with another person at your school or club to practice making phone calls for dif-ferent reasons..

Using Phone Books and Voice Mail to Get Information

1. Decide what information you need and write it down on a piece of paper.
Keep the paper and pencil with you.

2. The different sections of the phone book are color coded to help you in your search for information.

A) Look in the "yellow pages" of the phone book to search by category (e.g. bowling alleys.)

B) Use the "pink pages" to look for the names of businesses (e.g. Brunswich Bowling Lanes) listed in alphabetical order.

C) Use the "white pages" to look for numbers of specific people (e.g. Mr. W. Winner) listed in alphabetical order by their family names.

3. Before you call, plan what information you need to ask and what information you might be asked.

Be prepared to ask and answer these questions. For example, when you are asking about the costs at the bowling alley, someone might ask, "Do you own your own shoes?" (meaning bowling shoes).

Someone might ask you a question you are not prepared for. If you need more time to think about your response, just ask him or her to repeat the question to delay having to answer it.

4. Dial the phone number.

At this point a real person may answer or you may get a recorded message. The recorded message will likely give you lots of choices describing different types of information you might want.

If you listen carefully, the recorded message will give you the information you need (e.g. store hours, location, etc.) It will tell you to push different numbers to get different types of information.

If it is hard to listen or you get confused, you can usually push "0" after the automatic voice starts. "0" often takes you to the operator who is a real person you can talk with. However, sometimes you are put on hold for a long time before you get a chance to speak with the operator.

5. Once you get your information, you have to decide if the information is what you wanted or if you still need to talk with someone else to get answers to all of your questions.

What questions do you still have?

_____

_____

Making Phone Calls: The Plan

Page 1 of 2

You need to make a phone call to a person you know from your social thinking group to plan to do something with him or her or just to talk to that person about something of interest.

1. Who are you going to call? _____

2. Plan to get the person's number while you are around him or her. What would you say to get someone's phone number? (Hint: You likely want to say more than "I want your phone number." since people would wonder why you want it if that is all you say.)

    _____

    _____

3. Write out what you are going to ask the person on the phone.

    _____

    _____

4. Be prepared. Write down a question that person might ask you.

    _____

    _____

5. Stay Calm. Plan what you might talk about before you call to limit your worry that you will not know what to talk about. Remember to think about some things you know about the person you are calling. People like it when other people think about them.

© Michelle Garcia Winner 2005 • www.socialthinking.com

Making Phone Calls: The Plan

Page 2 of 2

6. Write down the information you learned during your phone call.

_____

_____

_____

_____

7. How does the information you learned help you make plans for what you can do together at school or at home?

_____

_____

_____

_____

8. Think about calling the person again. Friendships form when people show they are interested in the other person!

If an adult helped you with this, have that person sign here.

_____

Practicing Making Calls and Listening to Recorded Messages

Area Codes and Phone Numbers:

All phone numbers have 10 digits. The first 3 digits of a phone number are called an "area code" and when you write these you do it like this using parentheses:

(408) 888-8888

Big cities or regions often have many different area codes. For example, Zac, Nick, and Leanna all live within 20 miles of where their group meets, however they each have a different area code. Their area codes are determined by where they live in the region.

If I were to call Zac's house I would have to dial (650) first. If I were to call Nick's house, I would dial (510) and for Leanna, I would dial (831). Those numbers tell me the area that I am calling. The next 7 numbers then dial directly to the phone at the person's house or to the person's cell phone.

Often when you call a person who is in a different area code from yours, you are charged more for making the phone call.

When you call a person within your own area code you do not usually need to dial the area code. You only use the area code to dial a person outside your direct area code region. To let the phone company know you are going to call someone out of your area code, you always start by dialing a "1" before the area code and the phone number.

You will need to pay attention to dialing a "1" along with the area code and the phone number when you call people out of your area. You may also have to pay attention to how much this is costing you or your family. Your parents may ask you to not call people in certain area codes because it costs too much money.

Some businesses want you to call them to get information so that you will use their business. These people offer free telephone calls. The area codes for a free call are "800" and "866". These may change so make sure you find out which numbers are free before you call. It is important to know that not all businesses offer free area codes. Some businesses actually charge you a user fee each time you call their number in addition to what the phone company charges you to make the calls!"

Practicing Making Calls and Listening to Recorded Messages

Recorded Messages:

Most business phones today have "recorded messages." What is a "recorded message"?

_____

_____

Listening to "recorded messages" is tricky because they often list a number of choices. When you make a call and you get a recorded message:

1. Listen and take notes if needed.

2. Pick your choice.

3. Push the button that corresponds with your choice. Many times this takes you to a whole new recorded message so you have to be prepared to listen and choose a button all over again.

4. You can often avoid having to listen to the "recorded message" by pushing "0" which will usually take you directly to an operator. Try this if you just can't listen any more!

You try:

Start by finding an (800) number to a business like Disneyland or Disney World.

Listen to the recorded message and write down the choices that are offered:

_____

_____

Answer these questions by using the recorded messages:

How much does it cost for adults? _____

What age is considered to be an adult? _____

What hours is the business open? _____

Practicing Making Calls and Listening to Recorded Messages

Page 3 of 3

Recorded Messages (continued):

Is there another number to call? _____

Now try another number. Call a bowling alley in a nearby area with a different area code from your own!   (_____) _____
                    area code   *phone number*

Cost: _____

Operating Hours: _____

Cost of a Season Pass: _____

What button do you punch to get an operator? _____

Now try a number which has the same area code as yours.

Call a movie theatre in your area!   (_____) _____
                   area code   *phone number*

Call the movie theatre and find out what movies are playing at about 7 p.m. and how much they cost.

_____

_____

_____

_____

Great Job!

Dear _____ February 14, _____

Today is a great day to tell you that
I appreciate how you help me.

Thanks for helping me when I feel _____.

I want you to know that I feel _____
_____ about you!

Happy Valentine's Day!

From,

_____

Section 7

Understanding and Interpreting Emotions

My Mood Monitor

"Happy" - I feel great. When I feel great I am more flexible and I can see things from other people's point of view!

"Pretty good" - I feel pretty good. Things are fine and I can think about other people's needs as well as my own.

"OK" - Things could be better. I am just doing what I am told, but I don't like to be told to do too much! I know people have different points of view, but it's not easy for me to think about other people right now.

"Irritated" - I don't feel very good. I am getting moody and I don't see why every one is bugging me so much. It's hard for me to understand how other people are feeling or thinking when I don't feel very good.

"Angry" - I am mad. Things are not going the way I want them to. I think other people are making my life harder! I can't see why everyone wants so much from me! It is very hard for me to think about how other people feel right now!

Emotions are Shared by All!

All people have feelings. Having strong feelings sometimes is normal in all people whether the feelings are good or bad, happy or sad. What can make you feel strong happy emotions?

    1. _____

    2. _____

    3. _____

What makes you feel strong sad emotions?

    1. _____

    2. _____

    3. _____

People who share experiences often share emotions without even talking about them. For example, on September 11th 2001, almost all people in America were confused, sad, and angry. What are some other events that might cause groups of people to share the same feelings?

    1. _____

    2. _____

    3. _____

Emotions are Shared by All!

Page 2 of 2

People can also feel the same type of emotions at different times. When would people that you know have the following emotions?

Anger

Frustration

Jealousy

Sadness

Excitement

Disappointment

People express their emotions in different ways. Some people talk about them and some people show them through their behavior. Some people do both. People can "read" other people's emotions.

How do you express your emotions?

_____

How does your mom express her emotions?

_____

How Are You Feeling Today?

Name_____   Date_____

Draw a face to match each description.

Happy	Okay	Excited
Sad	Frustrated	Angry

Write about how you feel right now.

Which of the above feelings are you having right now? _____
_____

Why do you have this feeling? _____
_____

Emotions are not only things we feel, but also things we can talk about.
Describe to another person how you feel right now, and why you feel that way.

_____

Name two other feelings you have had today. Usually we have a whole bunch of emotions each day.

_____

Telling people how we feel helps them to understand our behavior. We can also help ourselves when we tell people how we feel since people can then better understand us and what we need at that moment. **Describe to your teacher how you felt when you last got upset and why you felt that way.** Practice explaining how you felt in a calm voice to help your teacher understand without him or her feeling like you are mad at him or her now.

Emotions Can Be Contagious

Emotions are like germs; you can spread them!

People catch each other's emotions and start to feel them themselves. Have you ever thought about the fact that when you are with happy people, they often start to make you feel happy too? How about when you are with someone who is angry? How does that start to make you feel?

Emotions are like germs; they are contagious!

Sometimes the emotion is a good germ; emotions that make other people feel happy should be spread all around.

Sometimes emotions are the unpleasant germs that spread and make other people feel bad.

We cannot easily control our emotions, but we can learn to control how we show them!

All people have their own ways they feel about certain things. No one can tell you NOT to feel the way you do, but people can ask you not to show your feelings so clearly. Sad emotions can bring people down and very good emotions can make people act silly during serious moments.

Sometimes we even hide our feelings... just so that we don't spread around the emotions germ.

When you are with a group of friends or working together in a classroom, there are times when you do NOT like what is happening in the group. Maybe you do not get to choose the activity, go first, or win the game... and you can feel frustrated. But if you want people to still want you to be in the group, you can't make your frustration contagious.

What would you do to make people THINK you are okay, even if you don't feel happy about what is going on?

_____

_____

PS: It is important to remember that we don't ALWAYS want to hide our emotions. As we grow up, we learn when it is a good time to share our emotions and when it is a good time to hide them.

Double Dip Feelings

Feelings can get pretty confusing! Sometimes you can have two very different feelings at once! Think of times when you felt "happy and sad", "playful and mad", "proud and scared", etc. at the same time. Write down why you had each pair of different feelings. Describing our feelings helps make them less confusing![1]

HAPPY AND SAD	
PLAYFUL AND MAD	
PROUD AND SCARED	
BRAVE AND AFRAID	
MEAN AND FRIENDLY	
EXCITED AND WORRIED	
HATED AND LOVED	

[1] Lesson adapted from the book *Double Dip Feelings,* Magination Press (2001)

Feelings When Playing Games

Each of us has feelings. We always should have at least one feeling about what is going on around us.

Read the actions below. Think about how you would feel if someone treated you in each of these ways. Draw a line from each action to the feeling you would likely have.

Someone you are playing a game with…

- says "I win!"
- says "you lose!"
- touches other people's game pieces.
- only touches his or her own game piece.
- doesn't look to see when it is your turn.
- watches the game and knows when it is his or her turn.
- says that he or she wants someone else to have bad luck.
- says that other people are doing a "good job."
- thinks mean thoughts but doesn't say them out loud.
- changes the rules to help himself or herself during a turn.
- follows the rules that the group plays by.
- yells at a person to take his or her turn.
- calmly tells a person it is his or her turn.
- tells someone else that he or she doesn't want to play with that person.
- tells someone else that he or she likes to play with that person.
- tells someone he or she should not win.
- says it is a dumb game because it only requires luck to win.
- announces the game is not fair.
- says, "I am not having very good luck!" if he or she is losing.

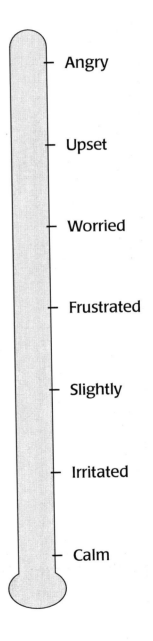

Angry

Upset

Worried

Frustrated

Slightly

Irritated

Calm

At what point on the "Emotions Thermometer" do you not want to play with someone anymore?

Read through the above actions again and circle those that you do well when you play with another person.

Playing can be hard work. We each have to work at being aware of how our behavior makes other people feel.

Matching Experiences to Emotions

Consider all the things that you have experienced in the past week, month or year and write down an experience you have had to match each emotion below.

Feeling fine:	Feeling good:	Feeling bummed:	Feeling relief:
Feeling frustrated:	Looking forward to something happening:	Feeling embarrassed:	Feeling nervous about something people expect you to do well:
Feeling over-whelmed:	Feeling proud:	Feeling someone was rude to you:	Feeling obnoxious or goofy:
Feeling angry:	Feeling excited:	Feeling that some-one was unfair to you:	Feeling weary or tired:

Now that you have identified experiences to go with each emotion, talk about each experience while matching your facial expression to the emotion in order to help people understand your words.

When you can do that well, describe a number of your experiences in succession and work at having your face show your feelings as you talk about each one of them. We are working on demonstrating a range of facial expressions during a discussion.

The videotape will help to provide feedback about how you are doing.

Feelings of Superiority…
Feelings of Disaster…Feelings of Others…

Page 1 of 2

Winning and losing can make us feel very weird!

There are lots of different words to explain how we feel when things are going well:
"superior," "fantastic," "terrific," "happy"

There are also words to use when things are not going well:
"horrible," "sad," "lonely," "awful"

And then there are words for feeling okay even if things aren't going perfectly:
"fine," "good," "okay," "satisfied"

When we play games with other people, there can be many different feelings that each person might have. Part of our job in agreeing to play a game is to make sure that we are not only thinking about our own feelings, but thinking about the feelings of others, too.

Sometimes how we show our feelings can change the way other people are feeling.

• If you show that you feel "superior," how does that make other people feel?

• If you show that you feel "horrible," how do other people feel?

• If you show that you feel "fine," how do other people feel?

Playing games should be fun. One hour after a game, how much will it matter who won or who lost? Do people really remember?

Aside from having fun with the people you are playing with, what is the job of the winner?

Feelings of Superiority...
Feelings of Disaster...Feelings of Others...

Page 2 of 2

Are people really "smarter" if they beat someone else in a game? Is the job of the winner to make the loser feel dumb?

What is the job of the loser? Should that person make the other people feel terrible that they lost the game?

Learning to control how we show our emotions is something that all people have to be able to do when they play, live, and learn with other people.

How can you control how you show your emotions???

1. First you have to know how you are showing your feelings.

2. Then you have to think about how other people might feel about the emotions you are showing.

3. If you think they might feel bad because of how you are behaving, you have to change how you show your feelings so that people keep wanting to be around you.

When I win a game, I feel _____.

And I want other people to feel _____.

So I can control how I show my feelings by _____.

When I lose a game, I feel _____.

And I want other people to feel _____.

So I can control how I show my feelings by _____

_____.

Embarrassment

By middle school most kids are strongly aware of being embarrassed by others or by doing things that would embarrass themselves. Teenagers often feel embarrassed by things that adults do not feel as embarrassed by. For example, teenagers get embarrassed really easily by the presence of their family (parents, brothers, sisters) when they are around their friends.

Embarrassment is defined as a feeling you have when you think that another person is having a bad or weird thought about you.

At times teenagers continue to participate in games or activities they don't enjoy just to keep people from having weird or bad thoughts about them.

A weird thought happens when people are thinking about the fact that you are doing some behaviors in a place where they are unexpected. For example, arguing with a teacher or refusing to do work in class can make people have a weird thought about you because it is unexpected.

You have weird or bad thoughts about others some times. Think about when you have had some of these thoughts in the following places:

Home

School

Store or Restaurant

Now think of other people in your family or your friends. When do they have a weird or bad thought about others…at home, at school or in a store, restaurant or movie theatre?

Teacher Notes

Section 8

Perspective Taking

What Do The Eyes Tell Us?

Page 1 of 2

Everyone says to use "eye-contact"... What does that mean?

When we look at people's eyes, we are supposed to get information from them. That means that when we watch someone's eyes we can get clues which help us guess at some of the things he or she is looking at and thinking about.

One way we can make these guesses is by looking in the direction the person's eyes are looking.

First look at the iris of the eye to determine the direction of the eye gaze. Then look at what the person is looking at and try to guess what he or she is thinking about. Is that person thinking about you? Someone else? Something else? (This may take some practice!)

Another reason we look at people's eyes and faces is to see the way peoples' eyes, eye-brows and mouths go together to make certain expressions. We call these facial expressions. Facial expressions give us more clues about what a person is thinking and feeling.

Looking at peoples' eyes also lets people know that we are interested in talking to THEM! That is why people say it is POLITE to look in peoples eyes. People want you to listen to them. But it is important to realize that not all cultures think it is polite to look into people's eyes. For example, people from the Asian or American Indian cultures may think it is disrespectful to look into the eyes of an adult. But in the United States, we generally think it shows respect to look at all people's eyes.

What Do The Eyes Tell Us?

Page 2 of 2

People look at your eyes too…

    1. If you are looking at them, then they think: _____

    2. If you are looking away from them, then they think: _____

Let's play a game during which different people take turns looking at something or someone and the other people in the room try to figure out what they are thinking about.

When you are with people, think with your eyes to figure out what they are thinking about with their EYES!

The Eye to Brain Connection

Detectives need to know that the way people's eyes move tell us a lot about what they are thinking.

Our eyes make tiny little movements in all different directions. Each little movement means our eyes are looking at something new.

Try this with a partner. One of you will be the "Looker" and one will be the "Watcher." The Looker will look at specific points on the partner. While the Looker is looking, the Watcher will watch how the Looker's eyes move.

1. Looker, start by looking at the Watcher's nose.

2. Now look at the Watcher's right ear.

3. Now look at the Watcher's left shoulder.

4. Now look at the Watcher's left ear.

Switch roles and do steps 1 through 4 again.

Watchers, did you see the Looker's eyes move? Were the eye movements great big movements or little tiny movements? How do people's thoughts change when their eyes move?

Now go back to your original roles.

1. Looker, look at the clock in the room.

2. Looker, look at the Watcher's shoes.

3. Looker, look at the Watcher's nose

4. Looker, look at the Watcher's left hand.

Switch roles and do steps 1 through 4 again.

What do you think? How did the eye movements differ?

What did the movements of the eyes tell you about what the Looker's brain was thinking about? (Hint: If you are looking at the clock, what are you usually thinking about?)

Now that we have practiced that, discuss this question in your group. What do you think eyes have to do with talking to other people?

© Michelle Garcia Winner 2005 • www.socialthinking.com

Two Terms: "Eye Contact" and "Thinking With Your Eyes"

When we ask people to use "eye-contact" we are encouraging them to look at us, but do people know that they should be thinking about what they see in other people's eyes and faces? When we use the term "eye contact" we generally assume that if you just look with your eyes you should know exactly what you are looking at.

When we use the term "think with your eyes" we give more direct information about what you should do with your eyes. "Think with your eyes" means you should look at other people's facial expressions and the direction of their eye-gaze to get you more information about what they might be thinking or feeling.

Think about the difference between the two terms, "thinking with your eyes" and "eye-contact."

1. What do you do with your eyes when people tell you to use "eye-contact?"

2. When people tell you to "think with your eyes," why should you be thinking about the other person?

3. Why does "thinking with your eyes" help you to better understand what someone is saying?

4. Why does "thinking with your eyes" help you to better understand what someone is feeling?

5. Why does "thinking with your eyes" help you to better understand what someone is paying attention to?

When you hear the term "eye contact," think about the fact that you should be "thinking with your eyes!"

Watching Versus Staring

Thinking with your eyes is a good way to know about the people around you and what is going on in the environment. However, some of the time we look at things without really thinking about what we are seeing. Often people can tell when we are "watching" things versus when we are doing a "blank stare." Think about these two terms and how you can tell the difference on other people.

Now think about whether people can see the difference between these two ways you use your eyes when they look at you.

"Watching" or "Observing" equals "Looking and Thinking"

Watching is when you pay attention to all the information around you to try to figure something out! Watching often involves listening carefully as well. For example, when you "watch TV" you are also listening to it.

"Blank Stares" equals "Looking and Not Thinking," which equals "Lost in Thought"

Blank stares are what your eyes do when you are lost in thought in your head and not paying attention to the information around you.

Earthling Tracker

B

What: Earthling Tracking is what we are calling our ability to sense when people are near us. When we sense people around us, we need to be thinking about why they are close. Do they want something from us? What are their intentions? (Or in other words "What's their plan?")

When: We should have our tracking device turned on ALL the time so that we are always aware of when others are near us.

Who: Everyone has a tracking device but as we have seen, some people's tracking devices are malfunctioning. The people in this group are part of the SUPER EARTHLING TRACKING SQUAD and are working very hard to keep their devices tuned in all the time.

Where: Everywhere, ALL THE TIME

Why: Why do we humans need to be aware of others around us? There are lots of reasons. One reason is because others have thoughts about us all the time and we should be having thoughts about them too. We need to be aware of others and what they are thinking about us so that we can do things to keep them having "good thoughts" about us. We also need to be aware of others so we know what adjustments we need to make to improve the interaction or situation and so that we don't hurt them. (For example, someone is near you and he or she wants to pass you. When you sense that person, you will move out of his or her way and that improves the situation. Or if someone is near you and that person is indicating that he or she wants to play with you, you can invite that person to play, and you've improved the interaction.)

How: How do we do this tracking thing? Here are the steps:

1. **Always be on the look out** for others.

2. When you sense that people are near, **Look at Them.**

3. Next, **try to figure out what they are doing and "What's their plan?"**

4. When you figure out their plan, **Make an Adjustment.** (For example, if they are trying to walk by you, move out of their way; if they want to play with you, ask them to play.)

Created by Therapist Randi Dodge and her group of Earthlings.

Abstract Quote about Social Thinking

"If you could see the you that I see

when I see you seeing me,

you'd see yourself so differently.

Believe me."

Henry Rollins (musician)

195

People Think About Other People in All Kinds of Places!

(Page 1 of 2)

Because we know that people think about us, we need to figure out what people are thinking about us. We also have to consider if what they are thinking about us is what we want them to think about us.

Discuss as a group what the ideas above mean.

No person is perfect. All people do things once in a while that make people have weird thoughts about them. However, usually we do not want people to have weird thoughts about us. So we monitor our behavior and try to change it if we know it is making people have weird thoughts.

List five things we can do in the classroom and during free time that might make people have weird thoughts about us:

Things that make people have weird thoughts in the classroom	Things that make people have weird thoughts during free time (e.g. lunch)

People Think about Other People in All Kinds of Places!

(Page 2 of 2)

List five things we can do in the classroom and during free time that might make people have good thoughts about us:

Things that make people have GOOD thoughts in the classroom	Things that make people have GOOD thoughts during free time (e.g. lunch)

Now the question is this. How do we monitor and control our behavior to help shape other people's thoughts about us, while still allowing ourselves to feel like we can express our needs and ideas?

To do this we have to practice watching ourselves…and that does take practice!

197

Seeing Other People's Plans
Through Their Body Actions!

(Page 1 of 2)

We try to figure out what people are planning to do when they are around us. Sometimes we can figure this out based on what they tell us, but most of the time we figure out what people are planning to do based on what we can see by paying attention to their body actions. A "body action" is any action a person's body does that communicates a message. Sometimes a body action is as simple as walking in the direction of a desired object.

Activities for "Reading People's Plans"

1. Game for Reading People's Plans

Rules for playing the game:

• People who are acting out their plans are NOT allowed to talk.

• People who are acting out their plans must make sure people are paying attention to them before they show what they plan to do.

• People who are acting out their plans may need to repeat their body actions 2-3 times to help the other students understand their plans.

a. Have a student sit at a table and point to a desired object. The other students then "read" that person's plan.

b. Have students take turns moving in the direction of a desired object or start a familiar action but have them stop short of actually touching the object or completing the action. Coach the students to freeze their movements just before completing actions like those that follow. The other students then "read the plan."

    i. reaching for the telephone

    ii. reaching to open the door to walk out

    iii. reaching for a book

    iv. throwing a paper away in the garbage

Seeing Other People's Plans
Through Their Body Actions!

(Page 2 of 2)

Activities for "Reading People's Plans" (continued)

2. Take students onto the campus of your school and have them watch people walking down the corridor. By watching people's actions or the direction their bodies are going, can the students predict where the people are going? (bathroom, office, etc.)

3. If your group will follow safety rules, go to your school's parking lot or a nearby street to watch drivers in cars. Can the students see what the drivers are thinking about based on where their eyes are looking? (e.g. Are the drivers seeing/thinking about the pedestrians?) It is important to teach students that when they are crossing a street they should not just look to see whether a car is coming. What is more important to teach is that they should look to see whether the driver sees them. If the driver sees the pedestrian, then he or she should stop and wait for the pedestrian to cross. Teach the students to always wait until they see that the driver has seen them before they walk in front of a car.

Thinking about People...

Whenever you are around other people you are supposed to monitor them with your thoughts. This is true even if you are not talking to them and even if you do not know them.

Discuss:

1. When you are around people, do you have a choice to think about those people or not?

2. When you are near others, do they have a choice to think about you or not?

3. What does it mean to think about someone else? What do you notice when you think about people around you?

4. Can you think of any place where you don't have to think about who is around you?

5. What happens if you don't think about other people who are near you?

It is a fact that people are always thinking about people who are around them. Can you help people to have good thoughts about you? How?

Can you make people have weird thoughts about you? How?

When would you want people to have friendly but weird thoughts about you? (For example, sticking your tongue out at them when you are joking around)

When don't you want people to have weird thoughts about you?

Food for Thought

(Page 1 of 2)

How do people digest these actions?

Consider the situations below and describe what the other people might be thinking:

1. A girl stands near the girls she likes but she is turned away and looking away from the group while they all talk together.

2. A girl stands in the group and looks at the other girls but does not say very much.

3. A girl stares up at the sky when she is talking about her shoes.

4. A girl goes off by herself during lunch and then says that no one was being very nice to her.

Food for Thought

(Page 2 of 2)

How do people swallow these words?

People have thoughts about what you say. If you have to "eat your words" it means you may have to apologize or show you are sorry for what you said, or at least acknowledge that what you said was wrong. Read each of the following and decide if a) the girl should "eat her words" or b) her words would be digested well.

1. A girl is wearing some new clothing. A friend says, "I tried that shirt on but I didn't like it."

2. In class a girl states that everyone is really dumb because no one knows the answer to the question the teacher is asking.

3. A girl says, "I tried that shirt on. It didn't look good on me but I knew it would look good on someone else." (as she looks at the girl wearing the shirt)

4. A middle school girl gets the best grade in the class and turns to her classmates and asks what score they got.

5. A middle school girl gets the best grade in the class and she asks another person in the class if they want to work with her on an after-school project.

6. A girl asks everyone what grades they got on their tests and then she says that she got an "A."

7. A girl says that she is really smart and all her teachers like her.

8. A girl says that she likes school because she likes to see all her friends.

Different Types of Thoughts

People who are listening have different types of reactions to what is being said. The speaker has to make sure he or she explains things so that other people can understand. It is not good enough if only the speaker understands what he or she is talking about.

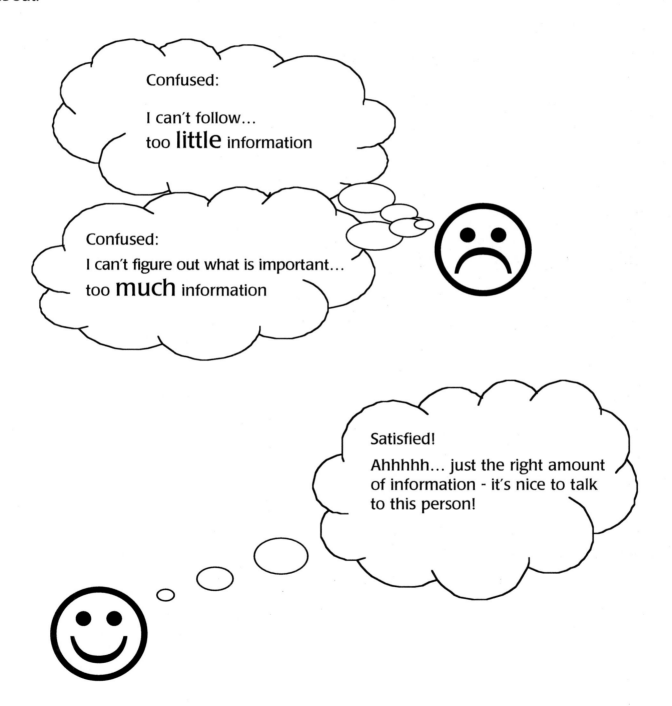

Confused:

I can't follow...
too **little** information

Confused:

I can't figure out what is important...
too **much** information

Satisfied!

Ahhhhh... just the right amount of information - it's nice to talk to this person!

Thinking About How People Think

We are going to play with ideas about being part of a group and thinking about others.

When we are part of a group we have to think about all the people that are around us. This means we have to have some rules. When people follow rules then other people continue to enjoy being with them.

Rules we can all live by:

Think about good rules for our group to follow so that we can all have fun together.

1.

2.

3.

4.

5.

When people don't follow the group rules, then people wish the rule-breakers were not in the group for a bit. What type of behaviors could happen that would make a child be asked to leave the group for two minutes??

1.

2.

People think, I think, you think, they think...

Different types of people expect different things from you. For example your teacher expects you to do a certain set of behaviors in the classroom but the yard duty person expects you to behave in a totally different way. You also expect different behavior from different types of people. What are the differences?

What are different behaviors you expect from...?

Teachers	Friends	Parents

What are different behaviors THEY expect from YOU?

Teachers	Friends	Parents

Would a teacher from school expect a different set of behaviors from you if she sees you at a holiday party that is not held at school? Yes _____   No _____

What behaviors would she now expect from you that are different from when she sees you in school? _____

_____

What behaviors would she expect to stay the same? _____

_____

WHY?_____

Learning about Social Thinking!

1. Thinking about how other people think

List 2 ways you use your eyes and ears to learn what other people are thinking!
1.
2.

2. Thinking about how other people think about you

List 2 ways you use your eyes and ears to learn what other people are thinking!
1.
2.

3. Behaviors that people expect and don't expect from you

Behaviors People Expect	Behaviors People Don't Expect!

4. Learning how to keep people happy when they are with you

List 2 ways you can keep people happy to be with you! (These should be things you are ready to try to do in real life!)
1.
2.

Thinking About How Others Think About You!

When do people think about you? _____

You Make Impressions:*

   1. By what you do

   2. By what you say

   3. By how you look

Write out what each means:

1. By what you say

_____

_____

2. By how you look

_____

_____

3. By what you do

_____

_____

Start watching others and tune into the impressions they make upon you!

Lesson derived from "Social Skills Strategies", Books A and B, www.thinkingpublications.com

You Are Always Making Impressions!

Parent initials _____   Date completed _____

Think of a time when you made a good impression:

Where?

Home

School

In the Community

This worksheet must be filled out with an adult. If you don't have any outings planned, politely ask your parents if they'll take you somewhere to practice making good impressions.

How did you make a good impression?

(For example, appropriately complimented someone, used good manners, did nice things for others)

Think of a time when you made a "not-so-great" impression:

Where?

Home

School

How did you make a "not-so-great" impression?

Section 8: Perspective Taking

Perspective Taking:
Putting Yourself in Their Shoes

Today we're going to pretend to be someone else. Your job is to sound like, look like, and think like the person or character on your card. Next you must answer questions the way you think that person or character would answer them. It's important for us to see things and think about things the way other people see them and think about them. This helps us understand them better. If we know how people are thinking, we can learn better ways to interact with them.

1. What's your favorite food?

2. What makes you happy at home or at school?

3. What do you expect from the other students at school or from the kids at home?

4. What do you expect students to do after school?

5. What do you think about students who do not follow the rules?

6. What is your idea of having a good time at school or home?

Your list of people or characters can include:

1. Mickey Mouse

2. Sponge Bob

3. My dad

4. My mom

5. My teacher of this class

6. My sister or brother

7. My principal

8. Another student in this social thinking group

Thinking About Others
Who Live In My House

Thinking about others includes thinking about people I live with. As I get older, I have more responsibility to the people I live with.

Household responsibilities I am supposed to do:

1.

2.

3.

These are things I know I should do to help. When I was younger I needed to be reminded a lot to do these things. Now that I am older, it is expected that I should have to be told no more than _____ time(s) before I do them.

When my folks have to tell me what they expect from me over and over again, I feel _____.

My parents also have feelings about this. They feel _____
_____.

I also have responsibilities to the social relationships I have in my house. I will define that as meaning: _____
_____.

Thinking About Others
Who Live In My House

Page 2 of 2

Here is a list of the people who live in my house and their particular interests:

1.

2.

3.

4.

Social relationships start with thinking about how other people think. This is called taking their perspective. When you think about others and question, compliment and comment about them, they usually feel more open to your own ideas. These are things we do to develop healthier social relationships.

Healthy social relationships are an important part of growing up because they help me to learn about: _____

_____

I can use the information above to help me develop more mature social relationships. Here are some ways I can use this information with the following people:

My mom

My dad

My brother or sister

Mom and Dad:
Who are these people?

Describe different aspects of your parents. We lump them together, but they are two very different people!

Mom   **Dad**

	With regard to: Appearance ←→	
	With regard to: Jobs ←→	
	With regard to: Enjoyments ←→	
	With regard to: Dreams/Goals ←→	
	With regard to: Their wishes for you ←→	
	With regard to: Their feelings ←→	

Point of View: Yours and Your Parent's

Page 1 of 2

Now that you are near adulthood, consider your point of view about the following.

1. Working at a job:

    a. wages desired

    b. what you use money for

    c. number of hours you should work each week

2. Use of your "free time:"

    a. amount of time you should have totally to yourself

    b. amount of time you should be doing responsibilities

3. Your responsibilities - List those that you think you should do:

4. What is your plan for eventually moving out of your parent's house?

Point of View: Yours and Your Parent's

What is your parent's point of view about you?

5. Working at a job:

    a. wages desired

    b. what you use the money for

    c. number of hours you should work

6. Use of your "free time:"

    a. amount of time you should have totally to yourself

    b. amount of time you should be doing responsibilities

7. Your responsibilities - List those that you think your parents want you to do:

8. What do you think your parent's plan is for you eventually moving out of your parent's house?

Feel free to discuss this with your parents!

A discussion like this is considered a sign of maturity.

Two Points of View!

When summer time comes, it is common that you and your parents have two different points of view about what you should do during your summer vacation. Write down thoughts about what your point of view is about this time and then consider and write down what your parents' point of view might be. It is likely that for some things you both share the same point of view and for other things your points of view are very different (for example, what time children should go to bed at night during summer).

Yours	Your Parents'

When people have two points of view, this can cause a problem...

Given that you and your parents probably have different ideas about summer vacation, think about this question. What is your possible problem and how will you work through it? (Hint: Use a problem solving worksheet.)

Point of View Worksheet:
Whose Point of View Gets Respect?

Page 1 of 2

What is a point of view?

People can have a point of view about anything that they choose to think about. Some points of view are imposed by law or moral code. List three of these:

1.

2.

3.

Some points of view make for interesting discussion, but are not of huge importance. Name two of these:

1.

2.

Some points of view have great importance to you, but perhaps not to others. Write down a point of view you have that others may not share.

When do points of view become cause for friction? List some points of view of others that can upset you.

1.

2.

Point of View Worksheet:
Whose Point of View Gets Respect?

Page 2 of 2

Each person has a point of view, but NOT all points of view are equal! In each of our homes, schools, and jobs there are some points of view that should not be openly discussed because they may be cause for an argument. There are people in most of our environments who help to lay the rules for which topics are "open for discussion," and which are not. Whose point of view takes the leadership role in the following settings?

Home:

School:

Work:

Why do these people get to have their point of view dictate the rules that are to be followed?

This really all comes back to the issue of respect. Why should these people have your respect?

What is respect?

While we are all taught to value our own points of view, you truly do not have a right to insist on yours in all environments.

When do you get to have your point of view take on more of a leadership role?

Someone Else's Point of View

Put yourself in your Mom or Dad's shoes...pretend you are one of them!

What responsibilities do you have during the day if you are your mom or dad?

1.

2.

3.

4.

What do you worry about?

1.

2.

3.

What do you expect from other people in the house?

1.

2.

3.

Now, jump back into your own shoes...

Given that you were thinking about your mom or dad's point of view...

What is one behavior that you think you could change because you know your mom or dad sees things differently than you do?

_____

Personalities...
WHO are the people we see?

"Don't judge a book by its cover."

Study of 3 characters from a TV show _____

Name:	Name:	Name:
Good attributes:	Good attributes:	Good attributes:
Not so nice attributes:	Not so nice attributes:	Not so nice attributes:
How does this character make you feel?	How does this character make you feel?	How does this character make you feel?
Describe the personality of the person:	Describe the personality of the person:	Describe the personality of the person:
How would you expect this person to behave at your work place?	How would you expect this person to behave at your work place?	How would you expect this person to behave at your work place?

B, C

Section 8: Perspective Taking

© Michelle Garcia Winner 2005 • www.socialthinking.com

Teacher Notes

Section 9

Making Plans to
Be With Others

Planning How to Get to Places in the Community

For Middle and High School Students

Page 1 of 2

When you were in elementary school, your parents were like taxi drivers. They drove you from one place to another and they did not expect you to pay attention to where you were going or how long it took to get there.

Now that you are an older kid, your parents are looking forward to the day when you can get yourself around town on your own by either driving or riding a bus. By the time you are in college or working in a job, you will want to be able to do this, and far more, without the help of anyone else. To get ready to move yourself around the community, you need to start paying attention to all the details involved. Then you will know how to plan to get where you are going, and get there on time.

Some basic tips:

1. Every time you get in the car to go somewhere, predict how long it will take to get where you are going.

2. If you anticipate it should take a certain amount of time when there is no traffic, make a smart guess about how much longer it will take during a peak traffic period.

3. Play a game with another person in the car during which you each guess how long it will take to get somewhere. How good are you at guessing? Do you tend to think you will get there sooner or later than you actually do?

4. Ask your parents questions to find out how many miles you will be traveling, how bad the traffic might be, and how long they think it will take to get you to where you are going.

5. Look out the front window and figure out if you know where you are. What are some of the landmarks you see on your trip?

6. If your travel plans include getting a ride home from someone else, you need to think not only about how long it takes you to get home from where you want to be picked up, but also how long it will take for your parent or friend to come and get you. For example, if you want to be picked up at 4 pm, you need to figure out what time to call your parent or friend so that he or she can pick you up on time.

Planning How to Get to Places in the Community

For Middle and High School Students

Page 2 of 2

Fill in the answers to these questions:

1. How many minutes does it take for you to drive to school? _____

   What time does school start? _____

   What time do you have to leave home by? _____

2. How many minutes does it take for you to go to the local mall? _____

   If you need to meet a friend there at 12 pm on a Saturday, what time do you need to leave your house? _____

3. How many minutes does it take for you to get to the movie theatre? _____

   If the movie starts at 7 pm, what time do you have to leave your house? _____

4. If you are meeting a friend at the theater, what time should you meet him or her? _____ This means you need to leave your house at _____.

5. If your parents are going to pick you up when the movie ends, and the movie lasts an hour and a half, what time do you need to tell your parents to pick you up? _____

   When and how do you let your parents know when to pick you up?

   _____

   What else should you tell your parents so that they can easily find you at the theater?

   _____

Plan to Go Somewhere Special

Page 1 of 3

There are at least 9 factors to consider when planning to go somewhere special:

1. Location and description of event

2. Planning around time - determine the date of the event and time it will take to get to the event, enjoy it and return back

3. Transportation to and from the event

4. Money - budget to enjoy the event

5. Communication with parents so they get you where you need to be, when you need to be there

6. Communication with people at your school or club so that they know where your group will be

7. Social - Who are you going with?

8. Are there any special things you need to bring? (For example, socks for bowling.)

9. What possible problems can happen on the trip? What are possible solutions we need to think about? (Discuss this as a group.)

Make some guesses about anything else you need to figure out before you can set your plans. Use the chart on the next page to help you plan to find the information.

Plan to Go Somewhere Special

Page 2 of 3

What do you need to find out?	How are you going to find it out?
1.	
2.	
3.	

Now that you have all the information you need write out the details of the outing making sure you include information about the 9 areas on the previous page:

1. Who is going?

_____

2. Where are you going?

_____

3. Where is the event and how long will it last?

_____

4. How much money do you need? (Always plan to take a little more than needed in case of emergencies.)

_____

5. How are you getting to the event? (Transportation)

_____

Plan to Go Somewhere Special

Page 3 of 3

6. Is there anything special that you need to bring?

_____

7. What forms do your parents need to read? Do they need to sign a form?
   If so, which form?

_____

8. If you have a form signed by your parents, who will you turn it in to?
   When will you do this?

_____

_____

9. How will you let people at your school or community group know where you all are
   going in case someone is trying to find you?

_____

_____

**Planning takes time but it helps everything to run smoothly so there will be few if any
surprises! Then we can all enjoy ourselves.**

227

All the Little Steps in Planning

You have worked before on making plans for field trips. What steps from those plans do you remember?

We are going on a field trip to _____

What are all the little pieces of information we need to figure out so that we can go on the trip as a group? Please list everything we need to find out or do in order to be able to go on this trip.

(Hint: Remember there are at least 9 factors to consider.)

1. _____

2. _____

3. _____

4. _____

5. _____

6. _____

7. _____

8. _____

9. _____

10. _____

Are there more?

Planning and Organizing, Even For Stuff At Home

Explore planning for fun things and for not-so-fun things to do during your free time

When you have "free time" at home it is important for you to "fill it" mostly with activities that you enjoy. But you also have to use your free time to do things (chores) to help other people who live in your house.

Plan what things you can do during your free time tomorrow.

1. List an activity that you enjoy. Write down how much time you will spend doing that activity.

_____

2. List an activity (chore) that you will do for your parents. How much time will you spend doing that activity?

_____

Now that you have chosen some activities you have some planning to do...

1. Which one should you do first? (Often we pick the one we least want to do.)

_____

2. Make a schedule based on how much time each activity will take. This helps you to plan ahead so that time does not just slip away and you don't get to do anything at all, fun or not so fun.

Time _____ Activity _____

Time _____ Activity _____

Planning a Free Time Activity

1. What is the activity? _____

2. What special tools or equipment do I need to do this? Do we have them at home or
   do I need to talk to my parents about getting them?

   Items needed to do the task:

   _____

   If I need to talk to one of my parents about an item needed, when do I plan to talk to
   him or her? _____

3. Is there a friend I could do this activity with that would make it more fun?

   Who should I call?_____

   When?_____

   If the activity will take more than one day, what is the next time/day I can get back to
   it? _____

Congratulations, you just made a plan! Now you have to follow through and do it!
This is called being responsible.

Let's do it!
Making Plans with Friends

I will feel so good when I get to do some things with my friends. One of my favorite things to do is: _____

I have to plan to do things with my friends. Even fun things require me to spend some time planning ahead.

Planning to Have Fun:

1. Who will I call? _____

2. When will I call him/her? _____

3. What is the plan? Ask your friend for his/her ideas about the following and then come to an agreement about what to do.

   • Where to go: _____

   • What to do: _____

   • When to do it: _____

4. What to talk about: Remember some things that person likes to talk about:
   _____

5. What if he/she can't do it? Then what should I do?

   _____

When I call people or talk to them at school and make plans, I feel good because

_____.

Sharing Group Party Planning

(Page 1 of 2)

1. When should we have a party? What day and time?

_____

2. What do we need? Make a list of five things…

    A. _____

    B. _____

    C. _____

    D. _____

    E. _____

3. Who should bring what? _____

_____

4. What should we play at the party? _____

_____

5. What are good things to talk about at a party? _____

_____

Sharing Group Party Planning

Even parties require plans…

Write out the plan!

1. _____
_____
_____

2. _____
_____
_____

3. _____
_____
_____

4. _____
_____
_____

5. _____
_____
_____

Have Fun!

Let's Do Lunch!

Interviewing and thinking about the person for whom you are to prepare food

We thought that it would be very special if everyone made lunch for someone in the group. We will draw names and you will be responsible for preparing a suitable lunch for the person whose name you choose.

The goal is to make a lunch that makes the other person feel good because you spent time thinking about them and preparing the food for them.

When interviewing the person you are to make lunch for, ask questions to obtain the following information. (Ask the teacher for help if you are not sure what questions to ask!)

_____ will make lunch for _____

Favorite Sandwich _____

Favorite things he/she likes on the sandwich _____

_____

Favorite Fruit _____

Favorite Chips _____

Favorite Dessert _____

Favorite Drink _____

What do you remember about this person's hobbies?

How can you decorate his or her napkin or lunch bag?

Have fun!

Making Plans for a Holiday Party

We need to cooperate together and plan what people are going to bring to the holiday party.

We know we need:

    1. Supplies to eat the food with

    2. Food

    3. Drinks

4 . Games (Teacher can supply)

Please write down what each person is planning to bring.

_____ will bring: _____

_____ will bring: _____

_____ will bring: _____

_____ will bring: _____

Even on fun days when we have parties, all of the people still have to be "Thinking about You" people. "Just Me" people make the party NO Fun.

How does it help the party if you are a "Thinking of You" person? Give one example.

_____

How does it hurt the party if someone is a "Just ME" person? Give one example.

_____

235

Initial Agenda for Voluntary Parent/Teacher Education and Support Meeting

This agenda is used to help get parent/teacher education and support meetings off the ground. The purpose of the meetings is to share information in a confidential forum and facilitate parent/teacher team building in order to better serve the student in both the home and school environments.

Typically these meetings will involve one hour of parent education about social cognitive deficits and how they are being addressed at school and one hour during which the parents speak about the joys and challenges of parenting their child. The goal is for all persons in attendance to gain new information and learn new skills to explore with the student.

Time: _____ Date:_____

1. INTRODUCTION OF PARTICIPANTS

2. PURPOSE FOR COMING TOGETHER
   a. We are all volunteering our time to build a team to help the student.
   b. The focus will be on problem solving and creating support for the student both at school and at home.
   c. The team will discuss how to talk to the student about his/her strengths and weaknesses.

3. PARENTS PERSPECTIVE
   a. Joys and challenges of your child – your perspective
   b. What are you doing at home? How do you follow the IEP at home?
   c. Brief overview of your expectations for your child at home
   d. Strategies which work at home that could help at school
   e. What do you want from the school?
   f. Building routines that stress responsibility

4. PERSPECTIVE FROM SCHOOL
   a. How to link the school and home experience
   b. Issues of serving this student at school
   c. Problem solving as parents and professionals: how are we working together?

4. WRAP-UP
   a. Should we proceed with setting up future meetings?
   b. What topics would you specifically like to discuss during the next meeting?
   c. When should the next meeting be? Best time and place? (August, before school starts?)

Section 10

Problem Solving and Dealing with Responsibilities

Solving Problems
Before They Become Problems

Page 1 of 2

1. What is the problem?

_____

2. Who is it a problem for, and why?

_____

3. What behavior choices do you have for solving the problem?

1. The bad choice	2.	3.

4. Write in possible consequences of each choice:

1a.	2a.	3a.
1b.	2b.	3b.
1c.	2c.	3c.

Solving Problems
Before They Become Problems

Page 2 of 2

5. What choice or choices are best to pick? _____

_____

6. When are you going to start to solve your problem? (List the date and time)

_____

_____

7. Where are you going to do this? (Location)time)

_____

_____

8. Who do you need to talk to, to get help? (Person)

_____

_____

9. What are you going to say or ask?

_____

_____

Problem Solving Does Not Always Result in Roses

Thoughts on Problem Solving:

• Ideally, you should anticipate your problems, and develop and carry through with your solutions before they become problems!

• If you actually have a real problem, then you have even harder choices to make. Why is it harder to solve a problem that you already have?

_____

• You need to consider other people's point of view to better understand your problem. This will help you determine the best way to solve the problem for everyone involved.

On the "Solving Problems Before They Become Problems" worksheet:

• You need to list at least 3 action choices for each potential problem.

• You need to decide which choice(s) you will act on depending on which consequence(s) you desire.

• You have to follow through after your good thinking and actually DO SOMETHING differently to help you solve the problem.

Solving Problems Does NOT Guarantee…

• that you will actually be happy with the results.

• that you will want to do what you have to do.

• that you will not still have a problem or frustration. It just guarantees that your problem or frustration will not be AS BIG as it could have been.

Good problem solvers focus on the long-term outcome of their action, rather than on the short-term action that they have to do to solve the problem.

Good problem solvers still have problems. No one is problem free. But by making good choices and following through with them, good problem solvers are more "successful." People perceive them positively, they may do better, and others want to work with them.

How do you make yourself focus on the long-term reward rather than the short term task to solve a problem? _____

_____

How to Figure Out If You Have a Problem

Red Flags

• You are blaming others.

• Other people let you know that things have to change.

• If you look down the tunnel, what you see at the end is not what you wanted.

• Even when you try to do something different, you still have a problem.

• Other people tell you they are disappointed in you.

• People are yelling at you.

• People are avoiding you.

• You feel upset on the inside but can't figure out why.

If you don't recognize these Red Flags...

• Then comes the "Yuck, I'm Stuck" phase:

It seems like too much work to do anything different.

• Then comes the "Damn, I'm in a Jam" phase:

It seems too late to do very much.

• Then comes the "Double Whopper Combo" phase:

Now you have twice as many problems.

Recognizing When Problems Are Mounting During Studies

Problems are something we should look for on a daily basis. The best way to deal with a problem is to deal with it before it explodes into a bigger problem. Some problems can be little glitches, but at times small glitches, if left untreated, can become more like volcanic eruptions.

Fill out the following chart:

Consider each of the following.	Describe what it looks like when Things Are Going Well.	Describe what it looks like when Things Haven't Gone Well.
Productivity Goal: What do I want to accomplish? How much time do I want to spend on it?	How much am I accomplishing? How long is it taking?	What is happening instead of meeting my productivity goal?
Emotions: What feelings do I have when things are and aren't going well for meeting my productivity goal?		
Distractibility: What distracts me from meeting my productivity goal?		
What to do about distractions: • What should I tell myself? • What should I physically do?		

Rules and Responsibilities

Page 1 of 2

Name _____ Date _____

1. A RULE is something others tell you to do in order for people to be safe and work well together.

2. A Responsibility is something that you impose upon yourself knowing that it will make others around you feel good.

Rules and responsibilities are not always clearly stated. As people grow up the rules and responsibilities change.

Rules and responsibilities also change based on the places that you are in. For example, you have more rules and responsibilities to follow at the dinner table at home than you do when you are playing by yourself in your room.

Consider and discuss the following:

When do rules change?

When do responsibilities change?

How are Rules and Responsibilities similar?

List 3 rules that you have to follow at home:

1.

2.

3.

Rules and Responsibilities

Page 2 of 2

List 3 responsibilities that you have at home:

1.

2.

3.

List 3 rules that your friends expect you to follow.

1.

2.

3.

List 3 responsibilities you have toward your friends.

1.

2.

3.

List 3 rules that you have to follow in your classroom.

1.

2.

3.

List 3 responsibilities you are expected to follow in your classroom.

1.

2.

3.

Are rules more important than responsibilities? Discuss.

245

© Michelle Garcia Winner 2005 • www.socialthinking.com

Tracking School Responsibilities

Fill out the chart below listing all the responsibilities that relate to you being a good student. These include working well within the class, doing homework, and getting grades that show you are trying to think about the work the teacher is teaching.

In the right-hand column:

• Put a check next to a skill you are already doing.

• Put an "x" next to a skill you are working on getting better at doing.

• Put an "o" next to a skill that you almost never do.

List all the little steps involved in being a "responsible student."	Check = you do this already "x" = you do this sometimes "o" = you almost never do this

Summer Thinking…about Free Time

Summer is a great time to unwind a bit. It is a time when you usually have more free time.

Free Time does not always mean "fun time." Free Time means that you have time to make fun choices and you also have time to follow through with your responsibilities (even though you wish you did not have to). Using your Free Time well means having fun AND taking care of your responsibilities.

Find a balance between your relaxing activities and your responsibilities.

"Free Time" really means "unstructured time that has to be structured."

List activities that you can do during your Free Time to create some structure.

Fun Activities	**Responsibilities**
1.	1.
2.	2.
3.	3.
4.	4.

Now list a balanced set of activities to do during your Free Time tomorrow. Predict how long each of these activities will take. Which take more time, your fun activities or your responsibilities?

1.

2.

3.

4.

5.

6.

7.

Kids, Adults and Free Time

Free Time is a time that is not already planned out for you. When you are at school or a job, you are given a schedule. When you don't have a schedule your time is more "free." But what does "free" mean?

Write down four different types of fun activities that your mom and dad do with their free (un-scheduled) time.

1.

2.

3.

4.

Many activities your parents do during their free time are NOT fun. What are must-do activities that you see your mom and dad doing? List five.

1.

2.

3.

4.

5.

How do you schedule your free time so that you have fun time and time to do your "must-do" activities (responsibilities)?

Adults know that "free time" means a combination of responsibilities and fun activities.

What responsibilities do your parents wish they never had to do?
If you are not sure, ask them!

Persistence Pays Off

Page 1 of 2

Persistence is the ability to work hard at something even when it does not feel good to do it right at the moment you are working on it! We persist at something to work toward a goal or to just do the activity as part of a group.

Reasons we persist at things include the following:

1. It is what is expected in a particular environment.

2. It shows we are working as part of a group.

3. We understand that many things in our life are not enjoyable but we have to do them if we want to hold a job or be considered a worthwhile friend.

4. We can learn things even when they are hard for us.

Name 3 things you have done in the last day that required you to persist:

1._____

2._____

3._____

How do you feel when you have finished a task you have persisted at?

_____

How do your parents feel when they see you are persisting?

_____

What strategy do you use to help you keep persisting? (Hint: Some people focus on the fact that others will not give them a hard time if they persist. Some people focus on the fact that their work will finally be done if they just persist and get it finished.)

Persistence requires you to postpone receiving your pleasures. **What do you think this means?** Is it worth it? When is it worth it? When does it not appear to be worth it?

Persistence Pays Off

Some things, like waiting in line for a ride in Disneyland, are easy to persist at.

Name three other things that are easy to persist at:

1. _____

2. _____

3. _____

Some things are much harder to persist at. Name three things that are hard to persist at:

1. _____

2. _____

3. _____

What can you do to help yourself be more willing to persist at one of the things on your second list above?

When can you try this? _____

How will you know if you have done well at persisting?

_____

_____

Section 11

Poster Handouts
for Students

252

Social Behavior Map

Behaviors That Are EXPECTED For Learning as Part of a Group in the Classroom

Expected Behaviors	How They Make Others Feel	Natural Consequences You Experience	How You Feel About Yourself
Sit where the group is sitting.		Calm voices	
Keep your eyes on the teacher or what she is talking about.	Happy	Pleased look on peoples' faces	Good
Work on tasks the teacher assigns during work time.		People compliment or praise your behavior.	
Ask for help.	Proud	People may just let you work quietly so that you can work.	Calm
Touch only your own materials.		People might give you special opportunities or special tasks.	
Use fidgets to help keep your body calm.	Calm	Students want to work with you.	Happy
Keep your comments and questions focused on the class topic.			
Take out your book, pencil, and paper at the start of class.	Pleased	Students may want to hang out or play with you during non-work times.	Relieved
Write down your homework assignment.		You earn a break time for concentrating well.	
Put materials away at the end of class.	Successful	People laugh at something you say or do and they want to hang out with **you**.	Included
Monitor your talking time so that you participate as a member of the group: not too much nor too little.			
Monitor your use of humor so that it blends in with the class and does not stand out.			

Behaviors That Are UNEXPECTED For Learning as Part of a Group in the Classroom

Unexpected Behaviors	How They Make Others Feel	Natural Consequences You Experience	How You Feel About Yourself
Your body does not look like it is part of the group (e.g. wandering, body turned away from the group).		Tense faces	
Your eyes are not focused on the teacher or what she is referencing.	Frustrated	Angry or solemn sounding voices	Sad
Refusing to work; including sleeping.		People tell you what you should be doing (they nag you).	
NOT asking for help.	Annoyed	Students may not want to work with you.	Anxious
Body is not calm and you are doing things that distract yourself or others.	Irritated	Students may not choose to hang out or play with you.	Mad
Smelling or touching people.		You are sent out of the classroom.	
Talking about things of interest to you, but your comments do not closely add to the class topic.	Worried you are not learning as part of the group.	You do not get any special rewards.	Not included
Not getting materials out at the start of class.			
Not writing down your homework assignment.	Tense	People laugh at something you say or do but they do not want to hang out with you.	
Not putting materials where they belong at the end of class.			
Cracking jokes or laughing during work times, distracting others or yourself.			

253

Social Behavior Map

Behaviors That Are UNEXPECTED For...

Unexpected Behaviors	How They Make Others Feel	Natural Consequences You Experience	How You Feel About Yourself

Behaviors That Are EXPECTED For...

Expected Behaviors	How They Make Others Feel	Natural Consequences You Experience	How You Feel About Yourself

The Boring Moments...
We all have them!

What's EXPECTED!

- Keep your BODY AND EYES TURNED TOWARD the teacher or work group.
- Keep your COMMENTS FOCUSED on the topic.
- FIDGET OR DOODLE QUIETLY, without distracting others.
- Keep only CLASS WORK on your desk.
- Keep NEGATIVE THOUGHTS TO YOURSELF!
- STAY ALERT so that you can jump back into the discussion!
- Continue to SIT UP in your chair.
- Keep your HANDS AND YOUR FEET TO YOURSELF.

What's UNEXPECTED!

- WANDERING around the classroom.
- SLEEPING or looking like you are sleeping.
- DISTRACTING OTHERS with your body or words.
- TAKING TRIPS to the bathroom or pencil sharpener.
- TALKING about things NOT RELATED to the class work.
- TELLING other people WHAT THEY ARE DOING WRONG.
- READING BOOKS during class that are NOT RELATED TO CLASSWORK.
- TURNING your BODY AND EYES AWAY from the teacher or work group.
- ANNOUNCING that you are BORED OR THAT YOU ALREADY KNOW THE INFORMATION!

Being Part of a Classroom Requires Social Thinking

When you are around other people,
just SHARING SPACE, be a SOCIAL THINKER.

FOUR STEPS TO SOCIAL THINKING
When sharing space realize that:

Step 1:
ALL PEOPLE have LITTLE THOUGHTS
about the people around them.

Step 2:
ALL PEOPLE TRY TO FIGURE OUT "why are you
near me" and/or "why are you saying this to me"?

Step 3:
Then, since I know you are THINKING ABOUT ME I try to figure out "WHAT ARE YOU
THINKING ABOUT ME?"

Step 4:
SO....I MONITOR AND POSSIBLY MODIFY MY BEHAVIOR to keep YOU THINKING
ABOUT ME, the way I WANT YOU TO THINK ABOUT ME!

REMEMBER:

**You still are a SOCIAL THINKER when you are JUST STANDING IN
LINE or QUIETLY WORKING in class.**

Also by Michelle Garcia Winner
and Think Social Publishing, Inc.

Think Social! A Social Thinking Curriculum for School Aged Students

Inside Out! What Makes a Person with Social Cognitive Deficits Tick?

Thinking About YOU Thinking About ME, 2nd edition

Social Behavior Mapping:
Connecting Behavior, Emotions and Consequences Across the Day
Available in English and Spanish

Sticker Strategies: Practical Strategies to Encourage Social Thinking and Organization, 2nd edition

Superflex®... A Superhero Social Thinking® Curriculum

Superflex® takes on Rock Brain and the Team of Unthinkables©
(co-authored by Stephanie Madrigal)

Superflex® takes on Glassman and the Team of Unthinkables©
(co-authored by Stephanie Madrigal)

You are a Social Detective!
(co-authored by Pamela Crooke) Available in English, French, and Spanish

Strategies for Organization: Preparing for Homework and the Real World

Social Thinking Across the Home and School Day

Social Thinking Posters for Home and the Classroom

A Politically Incorrect Look at Evidence-based Practices and
Teaching Social Skills: A Literature Review and Discussion

Socially Curious and Curiously Social:
A Social Thinking Guidebook for Teens and Young Adults

We Can Make it Better! Stories©
By Elizabeth M. Delsandro

Please go to www.socialthinking.com for a full list of our products and resources.